The importance of economic literacy

T0317008

Petra Lietz/Dieter Kotte

The importance
of economic literacy

PETER LANG

Frankfurt am Main · Berlin · Bern · Bruxelles · New York · Oxford · Wien

Die Deutsche Bibliothek - CIP-Einheitsaufnahme

Lietz, Petra:

The importance of economic literacy / Petra Lietz/Dieter
Kotte. - Frankfurt am Main ; Berlin ; Bern ; Bruxelles ; New
York ; Oxford ; Wien : Lang, 2000
 ISBN 3-631-36161-0

ISBN 3-631-36161-0
US-ISBN 0-8204-4740-4

© Peter Lang GmbH
Europäischer Verlag der Wissenschaften
Frankfurt am Main 2000
All rights reserved.

Printed in Germany 1 2   4 5 6 7

Acknowledgments

This book would not have been possible without the assistance of many people. Conducting a large-scale school research project such as the Economic Literacy Survey - Queensland 1998 is a team effort. And the whole team needs to be thanked.

First and foremost, we are grateful to Central Queensland University and the Faculty of Business and Law which provided the financial assistance and administrative infrastructure for the data collection, the statistical analyses and, finally, the report writing.

But we are particularly indebted to all the participating students, teachers and school principals who made this survey a great success.

We thank Education Queensland and the Board of Senior Secondary School Studies for giving us the permission to conduct the assessment and for providing us with valuable background information.

Special thanks go to Mr Bruce McGregor from St. Brendan's College, Yeppoon, who spent a lot of his private time in assisting us to rate the Australian curricula. We thank Bruce also for his help in conducting the pilot survey in 1997 and to volunteer for the PC and internet testing.

Last, but certainly not least, we are very grateful for the continuing support we received from Mr Jeff Ellis, Faculty of Education and Creative Arts at Central Queensland University, throughout the whole project. Being married to Petra during this survey must have tested his patience. Thanks, Jeff!

Petra Lietz & Dieter Kotte, November 1999

Table of Contents

List of Tables

List of Figures

Preface

A quick guide through this book

Few people enjoy the luxury of having sufficient time to read through an entire book from cover to cover in the hope of coming across some information that might be useful to them.

Hence, this quick guide has been designed to assist readers in going straight to those sections that are of particular relevance to their role as:

 policy- and decision-makers

 educators (eg. school principals and teachers)

 researchers

A paragraph or section relevant to one or more of these groups of readers is preceded with the corresponding symbol(s). As a further tool, each symbol is shown below together with the page numbers on which it occurs.

 policy- and decision-makers
1, 4, 17, 19, 30, 35, 50, 56, 60, 84, 92, 111, 119, 121, 125, 128, 129

 educators
1-4, 14, 17, 19, 30, 35, 40, 45, 47, 50, 60, 62, 64, 65, 67, 68, 71, 73, 76, 78, 78, 84, 89, 92, 102, 105, 106, 111, 114, 118-121, 125-128

 researchers
1-4, 13, 17, 19, 24, 30, 32, 35, 46, 50, 54, 56, 60, 62, 64, 65, 67, 68, 71, 73, 76, 78, 82, 84-86, 89, 92, 96, 97, 102, 105-107, 111, 114, 118-121, 125, 127-129

Enjoy the read!

Petra Lietz & Dieter Kotte, November 1999

XV

Chapter 1

The importance of economic literacy

*"High school graduates will be making economic choices all their lives,
as breadwinners and consumers, and as citizens and voters.
A wide range of people will bombard them with economic information
and misinformation for their entire lives.
They will need some capacity for critical judgement."*

Nobel Laureate in Economics, James Tobin (1986)

 Economic literacy refers to an understanding of basic economic concepts which is necessary for members of society to make informed decisions not only about personal finance or private business strategies but also about the relative importance of differing political arguments. Walstad (1988, p. 327) operationalizes economic literacy as involving economic concepts that are mentioned in the daily national media including "tariffs and trade, economic growth and investment, inflation and unemployment; supply and demand, the federal budget deficit; and the like".

Rader (1996, p. 5) emphasizes the necessity of fostering economic literacy as follows:

> Students who do not understand the role of profits in an economic system may develop a negative attitude toward business. The lack of economic literacy leads to the existence of attitudes that may inhibit economic progress. […] economic literacy will lead to the making of better choices by our elected representatives, which in turn will lead to an improved quality of life for the large majority of our citizens.

Likewise, Ellison and Kallenbach (1996) consider economic literacy to be an important component of adult literacy. They argue that

1

without the development of students' awareness of the way in which political and economic decision-making occurs and may be influenced educators do not fulfil their brief of enabling "students to gain control over their lives" (Ellison and Kallenbach 1996, p. 26).

Therefore, the teaching of economics in schools has been argued by many authors (Gleason & Van Scyoc 1995; Huskey, Jackstadt & Goldsmith 1991; Walstad 1988) to be vital if students as future adults are to have a sound basis for evaluating economic information, which, in turn, will guide their electoral and business decisions.

  In Australia, the importance of economic literacy has been acknowledged through the introduction of Economics as an elective subject in the last two years of secondary schooling (Board of Senior Secondary School Studies 1992). The general thrust of the subject is reflected in the aims of the senior secondary school curriculum for Economics in Queensland (1995):

- For students to develop an understanding of economic principles and methods so that they may function more effectively as decision-makers in economic questions and more responsible as adult citizens.
- To replace emotional judgements by rational, objective methods in examining social and economic problems.
- To generate in students a lasting interest in Australian and world economic problems.
- For students to realise that economic problems change over time, that economic decisions taken in the past have developed the economy to its present state and that decisions will have to be made to meet new and probably more complex problems in the future.

Likewise, the Western Australian Economics syllabus for Year 11 (D304 syllabus, p. 23) states:

Economic literacy and the general level of community interest in economic matters have never been higher. Media treatment of economic issues, and especially debates by public figures has given economics a high profile.

This book provides a detailed account of prior research into economic literacy as well as the current state of Economics education.

The first chapter serves as a summary of prior research into economic achievement and ways in which economic literacy has previously been operationalized and assessed. Results of the studies allow insights into performance levels and factors associated with performance.

Chapters 1, 3 and 4 present the current state of Economics education in terms of the intended, implemented and attained curriculum put forward by Rosier and Keeves (1991) and Lokan, Ford and Greenwood (1996). In Chapter 2, a content analysis of the Economics curricula of all Australian States and Territories gives an overview of the intended curriculum in that it highlights what students are expected to learn during their studies of economics at the senior secondary school level.

Chapter 3 discusses the implemented Economics curriculum based on a Queensland wide survey undertaken in 1998. As part of the survey, school principals and teachers supplied information on different aspects of the implemented curriculum such as school equipment, class sizes, content foci, teaching materials, and instructional strategies.

Evidence from the same survey forms the basis of Chapter 4 which illustrates the attained curriculum in terms of levels of Economics achievement across all participating students. In addition, performance levels are compared across subgroups of students, for example, different school types, gender as well as rural and urban areas. At the same time, comparative data are presented regarding student performance in the different Economics content areas, namely Fundamental Economic Concepts, Microeconomics, Macroeconomics and International economics.

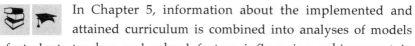 In Chapter 5, information about the implemented and attained curriculum is combined into analyses of models of student, teacher and school factors influencing achievement in Economics. On the basis of prior research, logic and chronology, models are developed and subsequently analyzed to generate evidence regarding the relative effects of different factors on each other and on Economics performance.

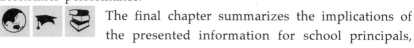 The final chapter summarizes the implications of the presented information for school principals, teachers, policy and decision makers and educational researchers who are interested in furthering Economics education at the senior secondary school level in order for students to become informed adults who are able to evaluate economic policies and decision making.

1.1 Operationalisation and assessment of economic literacy

Initial research on economic literacy was undertaken in the United States. Here, the *Joint Council on Economic Education (JCEE)* had been established in 1949 to increase the quantity and quality of economic education in schools. As part of its activities, the Council produced curricular outlines for schools of the content and cognitive categories of the subject of Economics. The documents included the *Economic education in the schools* (CED 1961) and the *Master curriculum guide in economics for the nation's schools, Part 1, A framework for teaching economics: Basic concepts* (Hansen et al 1977), which was revised in 1984 (Saunders et al 1984).

Concurrent to the curriculum documents, the JCEE developed tools aimed at assessing the specified content. Thus, the *Test of Economic Understanding (TEU)* was the first to be designed in 1964 (TEU 1964), followed by the first edition of the *Test of Economic Literacy (TEL)* (Soper 1978, 1979), which was subsequently updated (Soper & Walstad 1987).

The curricular framework authored by Saunders et al (1984) defined economic literacy as involving economic concepts that were mentioned in the daily national media. This was operationalized for construction of the TEL to include "tariffs and trade, economic growth and investment, inflation and unemployment; supply and demand, the federal budget deficit; and the like" (Walstad 1988, p. 327).

Test items in the TEL (Walstad & Soper 1987) covered four content categories: Fundamental economic concepts, macroeconomics, microeconomics and international economics. In addition, each item was assigned to one of five cognitive levels: Knowledge, comprehension, application, analysis and evaluation. The TEL consisted of two parallel forms, each requiring about 40 minutes of testing time.

The two parallel forms (Form A and Form B) of the TEL were administered in 213 high schools throughout the United States (Walstad & Soper 1987) in order to obtain norming data against which test administrators could compare results. Attention was given to select schools representing different geographical regions, rural and urban areas as well as school sizes. While no representative sampling was undertaken in the design phase of the study, results of a post-hoc analysis of the sample in terms of general ability (IQ), socio-economic status and ethnic-racial mix showed that students represented a cross-section of the US high school population from Grades 10 to 12. Table 1.1 provides information on the aggregate statistics for the TEL norming sample in the United States.

While the TEL was developed in the late Eighties, it is still being used where information on achievement levels in Economics is sought. For example, a recent study of 665 Grade 11 and 12 students in Athens County in Ohio using the TEL showed the highest performance in the area of microeconomics and the lowest performance in the area of international economics (Stock & Rader 1997). A comparison with the 1986 norming data of the TEL revealed that Grade 11 students in south-east Ohio achieved above the national

	Form A	Form B
Total number of students tested	4,235	3,970
Cronbach's α	0.87	0.88
Percent of students studying Economics	74.50	69.65
Mean overall	22.06 (8.33)	22.13 (8.68)
Mean and standard deviation - Students enrolled in Economics (N of students: Form A=3,153; Form B=2,765)	23.33 (8.45)	23.92 (8.85)
Mean and standard deviation - Students not enrolled Economics (N of students: Form A=1,082; Form B=1,205)	18.37 (6.71)	18.01 (6.64)

Note:
figures taken from Walstad & Soper 1987, p. 12; standard deviations in brackets

mean for that grade level while Grade 12 students performed significantly below the national average (Stock & Rader 1997).

The TEL has also been used outside the United States in an attempt to compare student achievement in Economics across countries. Thus, Whitehead and Halil (1991) administered the TEL in selected parts of the United Kingdom, where the test was valid in so far as it reflected the core elements of the British advanced-level Economics syllabus. The TEL was, however, adapted to the British context in terms of spelling and terminology (eg trade union → labor union, comprehensive school → public high school). Otherwise, the test remained unchanged.

An attempt to replicate the American sample as closely as possible proved difficult as strata that were used in the US such as region or type of community were argued to be meaningless in the UK. Furthermore, as a consequence of the high attrition rate of British students 16 years or older, the range of ability in the British sample was

Table 1.2:   *Aggregate statistics of the TEL for UK sample*

	Form A
Total number of students tested	7,610
Cronbach's α	0.77
Percent of students enrolled in Economics	57.00
Mean overall	30.09 (7.78)
Mean and standard deviation - Students enrolled in Economics (N of students: 4,311)	34.36 (5.28)
Mean and standard deviation - Students not enrolled in Economics (N of students: 3,238)	24.58 (6.26)

Note:

> *figures taken from Whitehead and Halil (1991, pp. 104+107); results are presented just for Form A as only this form was administered in this study; standard deviations in brackets*

assumed to be smaller than in the US sample. Hence, Whitehead and Halil (1991) asked for caution when comparing the results for the American and British students which are presented in Table 1.2.

In their endeavour to implement the TEL in Austria, Germany and Switzerland, Beck and Krumm (1989, 1990, 1991) were faced with considerable difficulties in terms of translation. This was mainly a result of the different sentence structures in English and German which had far-reaching implications for the wording of the distractors. However, a laborious process of translation and back-translation the researchers produced an equivalent test (Beck 1993).

In order to assess the content validity of the TEL, Beck and Krumm (1989, 1990) invited a national advisory committee of ten prominent economists to judge each test item on how good or poor an indicator of economic literacy in the German-speaking countries it would represent. While the experts agreed that the TEL measured some of what they considered to comprise economic literacy, they held

Table 1.3:   *Aggregate statistics of the TEL for Austrian sample*

	Form A	Form B
Total number of students tested	1,051	1,069
Cronbach's α	.83	.82
Percent of students studying Economics	na	na
Mean overall	20.09 (7.05)	21.67 (7.23)
Mean and standard deviation - Students enrolled in Economics (N of students: Form A=832; Form B=853)	20.47 (7.24)	22.07 (7.57)
Mean and standard deviation - Students not enrolled in Economics (N of students: Form A=219; Form B=216)	18.65 (6.07)	20.09 (5.42)

Notes:

   figures from Beck (1993, pp. 44+77). reliability coefficients (Cronbach's α) based on joint sample of German and Austrian students; standard deviation in brackets

na   not available

the view that the TEL stressed macroeconomic concepts at the expense of microeconomic concepts. In addition, it was argued that the skills believed to be 'basic' might not be sufficient in order to cope with the full range of economics issues (Beck 1993).

Following the required contextual changes to the original wording of the items and distractors a German version of the TEL, called *Wirtschaftliche Bildungs-Test (WBT)*, was administered to a sample of students in Germany and Austria between 1990 and 1991. For comparative purposes, Table 1.3 presents aggregate results for the Austrian subsample and Table 1.4 for the German subsample.

As a result of the study, Beck and Krumm (1989, p. 20) concluded:

> We are now confident that, by modifying the WBT (Wirtschaftliche Bildung Test) slightly, we will have an instrument that allows us to carry out valid cross-national comparisons no matter which aspect of economic literacy the instruments measure.

However, despite the efforts of Beck and Krumm to validate the test items of the German version of the TEL, the results collected in Germany and Austria could not be compared directly with those reported for the US and UK. Not only were the German speaking students tested in a different year than the American or British youth but the composition of the samples drawn could not be claimed to be representative for the whole of Germany and Austria since only a minority of states within these countries took part in the survey (Beck 1993, p. 34).

A selection of six questions from the TEL was also administered to a sample of high school students in Beijing, China (Shen & Shen 1993). The authors reported that 66.6 percent of students in the Chinese sample answered the questions correctly compared with 61.3 percent of student in the US national norming data set for the TEL. Similar to the argument put forward by Whitehead and Halil (1991) to explain the higher achievement of UK students, the higher achievement by the Chinese respondents was probably a result of a far more selective elite group of higher performers being retained at high school level in the Beijing-only sample (37% of the age cohort) compared with the large retention of high school students across the whole of the United States (95% of the age cohort).

Thus, in their summary of these applications of the TEL at the senior secondary school level in different countries, Walstad and Watts (1994) emphasized that the assessments in the different countries were not designed as a systematic cross-national survey with nationally representative samples at equivalent year levels. Nevertheless, they argued that the emerging differences in student performance levels reflected the different intensity and coverage of Economics as a school subject in the educational systems.

The *Test of Understanding in College Economics (TUCE)* (Saunders 1991) was designed specifically to assess Economics achievement at the post-secondary school level. In its third edition (TUCE III), the US developed test consisted of two instruments, one

	Form A	Form B
Total number of students tested	4,610	4,532
Cronbach's α	.83	.82
Percent of students studying Economics	na	na
Mean overall	20.57 (7.44)	22.27 (7.46)
Mean and standard deviation - Students enrolled in Economics (N of students: Form A=3,289; Form B=3,226)	20.86 (7.56)	22.63 (7.61)
Mean and standard deviation - Students not enrolled in Economics (N of students: Form A=1,321; Form B=1,306)	19.86 (7.09)	21.39 (6.99)

Notes:

figures from Beck (1993, pp. 44+77); reliability coefficients (Cronbach's α) based on the joint sample of German and Austrian students; standard deviation in brackets

na   not available

covering microeconomic concepts and the other dealing with macroeconomic concepts. Each instrument contained, in addition to its 30 core items, three questions regarding international economics and was designed to be completed by students within a 45 to 50 minute class session. Each item was assigned to one of three cognitive areas, namely, recognition and understanding, explicit application and implicit application. The explicitly stated emphasis of the test was on application (Saunders 1991, p. 33) and items were constructed from authentic materials. Due to its specifity directed at the US college system, the TUCE has not been administered in other countries.

Hence, the TEL remains the only instrument measuring levels of economic literacy to have been administered across different educational systems and found to be valid and reliable in different educational contexts.

1.2 Factors influencing economic literacy

While a comparison of achievement levels based on a national mean or across countries is of considerable interest, it is of equal if not greater relevance to educational practitioners and decision-makers to investigate possible reasons for differences in achievement levels between students and schools within countries.

An examination of different factors reflecting student and teacher background, instructional practices and school resources allows the examination of the way in which these factors may influence performance. This, in turn, permits educators and policy-makers to identify specific factors which can subsequently be changed in such a way as to increase performance levels. Factors which can be influenced by taking appropriate steps are known as *malleable variables* (Comber & Keeves 1973; Keeves 1996; Kotte 1992; Lietz 1996). The following sections provide a summary of research into malleable variables and factors influencing economic literacy. Since these factors can operate at various levels, differentiation is made between student-level factors and teacher- and school-level factors.

1.2.1 *Student-level factors*

As part of the norming process of the TEL in the United States, Walstad and Soper (1987) obtained information also on a number of student characteristics such as race, sex, type of community and income level. An examination of the mean raw scores for students on the TEL Form A (ie out of a maximum of 46 points) who had received formal instruction in Economics revealed the highest performance level for white students ($\bar{x}$=24.55 points), followed by other ($\bar{x}$=22.76), Hispanic ($\bar{x}$=21.37) and black students ($\bar{x}$=19.72). Male students performed at a higher level ($\bar{x}$=23.97) than female students ($\bar{x}$=22.68). Furthermore, rural students displayed the lowest average achievement ($\bar{x}$=19.41) while students in urban areas performed at a higher level ($\bar{x}$=23.81) and students in suburban locations showed the highest mean score ($\bar{x}$=26.01). In addition, students from low income families exhibited the lowest performance ($\bar{x}$=20.64), while students with high income backgrounds demonstrated higher performance ($\bar{x}$=24.31) and the highest mean score ($\bar{x}$=25.30) emerged for students from families with middle income levels.

Likewise, Whitehead and Halil (1991) reported mean performances for different subgroups in their norming sample for the United Kingdom. Here, mean raw scores for Grade 11 students with Economics education were recorded by sex as well as school type and area. Like the results in the US, higher scores were found for boys ($\bar{x}$=32.89) than for girls ($\bar{x}$=30.32). When scores where compared for different school types and areas, the highest mean achievement emerged for independent schools ($\bar{x}$=32.44), followed by London boroughs ($\bar{x}$=31.51) and home counties ($\bar{x}$=31.88) with the lowest mean achievement recorded for counties in the north of England ($\bar{x}$=30.98).

Analyses of the pilot study conducted to validate the WBT, as the German version of the TEL, indicated that the expected ranking of achievement levels of different subgroups was matched by the actual rankings that appeared in the data. Thus, students at universities ($\bar{x}$=34.18) performed better than students enrolled at the upper secondary school level ($\bar{x}$=27.32) and vocational schools ($\bar{x}$=22.43). Furthermore, the performance of students who read about economic issues in the newspaper was shown to be higher than that of students who did not read those newspaper sections (Beck 1993).

Walstad and Becker (1994) included sex, race and ethnic origin into two regression equations, one predicting microeconomic and one predicting macroeconomic performance. Results showed that none of these variables contributed significantly to the regression equation. However, these results were obtained *after* the score based on the multiple choice section of the test was entered into the equation and found to account for 90 percent of the variance in macroeconomics and 94 percent of the variance in microeconomics. Hence, the absence of any effects of sex, race and ethnic origin reported by Walstad and Becker (1994) on performance could be explained by the design of the regression analysis and should be treated with caution.

In a summary of research into economic literacy, Hallows and Becker (1994) stated that most studies undertaken in the US had not found any achievement differences as a consequence of student's race. In addition, they reported that achievement influenced attitudes to a greater extent than vice versa and that a gap between male and female performance emerged as early as Grade 5 and continued throughout high school and college with boys achieving consistently at higher levels than girls.

More recently, Gleason and Van Scyoc (1995) obtained information from 942 adults in Wisconsin who were currently not in college. While economic literacy levels were measured using the TEL, information was also collected on variables such as gender, whether or not they had studied Economics at high school and/or at college, age, educational level and family income level. Results of the regression analyses (Gleason & Van Scyoc 1995) showed that...

- males performed better than females;
- adults who had taken an Economics course at college performed at a higher level than adults who had not taken such a course;
- scores increased with age;
- adults with a higher educational level performed better.

The authors also concluded that...

- completion of a high school Economics course did not increase the score significantly. The authors hypothesized that economics can be learned by experience. Hence, age would have cancelled out any effect that completion of a high school Economics course might have had;
- both adults and high school students score higher on the microeconomics and fundamentals sections of the TEL than on the macroeconomics and international categories.

As is the case in other curriculum content areas (Keeves 1992[2]; Kotte 1992; Lietz 1996), student aptitude has been shown to be a powerful predictor of economic literacy. Indeed, Becker (1997, p. 1363) reported achievement measures at the beginning of a university Economics course to be "the only consistently significant and meaningful explanatory variable" of final achievement.

Sedaie (1998) undertook a secondary analysis of data obtained in the 1987 economics survey conducted by the National Assessment of Economic Education (NAEE). The analysis of the multinomial logit model revealed that students who indicated that Economics helped them to consider the advantages and disadvantages of pursuing further education had significantly greater intentions to attend college. This result emerged after effects of gender and race (both non-significant) as well as students' prior high school performance and parental education (both highly significant) had been taken into account in the model.

Schroeder (1998) reported similar attitudes of boys and girls towards a number of economic issues from a study of a representative sample of US students in Grades 9 to 11. Both male and female teenagers, who wanted to gain practical knowledge about finance and money matters (91%), were worried about their financial future (33%) and thought that level of education and level of earnings were linked. However, girls displayed greater apprehension than boys regarding the financing of their college education (37% cf 29%) and lower preparedness to invest in the stock-market (48% cf 64%). Moreover, twice as many boys as girls considered themselves very knowledgeable in money management (Schroeder 1998).

1.2.2 Teacher- and school-level factors

A national representative study of high school Economics teachers (Highsmith 1990) showed that the average Economics teacher in the US...

- had 16 years of teaching experience;
- had taught Economics for 6.5 years;
- held a Bachelor's degree;
- did not major in Economics but rather in subjects like Social Sciences, History or Education;
- also taught Social Studies;
- was white;
- was male and
- used graphs, charts and newspapers as instructional material.

Becker, Greene and Rosen (1990) as well as Hallows and Becker (1994) found that most studies on economic literacy in the US had provided evidence that teacher ability contributed considerably to student performance in Economics. However, inadequate teacher education in Economics was reported in Hallows and Becker's (1994) summary of research to remain a belief rather than a fact supported by any empirical evidence.

The relevance of the school subject of Economics to equip students with knowledge that is useful for future work and education is reflected in teachers' rankings of their goals when teaching Economics. Highsmith (1990, p. 82) reported that 90.2 percent of teachers ranked it as very important "to prepare students to make intelligent decisions as workers, consumers and voters". This was followed in importance by the objective to increase students' understanding of the American economy (89.1%) whereas teaching students about alternative economic systems received the lowest percentage of teachers considering it to be very important (18.5%).

Becker (1997) presented results of a survey of 625 undergraduate Economics lecturers which showed that half the respondents spent 83 percent of teaching time lecturing and writing on the blackboard, regardless of whether the university was teaching or research oriented. In contrast, whether or not lecturers employed cooperative learning techniques varied with the type of institution, with research institutions reporting no time while half of the lecturers at associate institutions, which focus on teaching, reported the use of this instructional strategy 22 percent of the time. Furthermore, lecturers illustrated economics concepts scarcely with examples taken from the literature (0-4%) and slightly more from sports (6%). The average lecturer reported using computer labs between 11 percent of the time in associate institutions and 34 percent in research institutions.

In a secondary analysis of data from the NAEE database, Grimes and Register (1990) examined the impact of different teacher background variables on Economics achievement with a particular focus on teacher's union status. For this purpose, unionization of teachers was introduced as an independent variable in the first block of a stepwise regression analysis. Subsequently, a block of independent variables labelled 'teacher inputs' - which included teaching experience, number of years teaching Economics, number of hours teacher took Economics at college, teacher enthusiasm, and teacher autonomy - was added to the regression model. Results showed that students taught by unionized teachers achieved at a higher level. In addition, teachers with (a) a greater number of hours of college Economics education, (b) greater autonomy, and, to a lesser extent, (c) more enthusiasm had students who displayed higher levels of performance. General teaching experience did not have the expected positive effect on achievement. Moreover, specific Economics teaching experience had a negative effect on achievement. A possible explanation put forward by Grimes and Register (1990) was that the TEL, which had been used to obtain performance data, had been recently revised to reflect curricular changes in the United States. Teachers who had taught Economics for longer might not have been aware of those changes, hence failing to teach their students the updated content required to perform well.

On the issue of class size, Becker (1997) contended that smaller classes facilitate the employing of different teaching strategies when teaching Economics. However, this stance appeared to be based on pedagogical theory rather than empirical evidence.

In a review of research on high school economic education, Becker, Greene and Rosen (1990) stated that little empirical evidence was available to support the claim that any of the tools provided by schools to support classroom teaching, such as, for example, special TV programs, flash cards, games and computer simulations had resulted in higher student performance.

Grimes and Register (1990) included a school's annual instructional cost per student as well as its enrolment in terms of number of students in a regression model predicting Economics performance. Results showed notable positive effects of both variables indicating that greater expenditure per student and a larger school size led to higher performance.

1.3   Summary

Economic literacy is of utmost importance as it represents an understanding of basic economic concepts which are vital for the critical evaluation of different options regarding study, work and private matters that people will encounter during their adult lives.

As a consequence, educators have to consider how students will develop into economically literate citizens. Studies in the US, Europe and China have found that there is room for improvement in terms of the economic literacy levels achieved by senior secondary school students. In addition, various student, teacher and school factors have been shown to influence achievement levels in Economics.

This book provides a detailed examination of the context in which Economics is taught and learnt in Australia in terms of the intended, implemented, and attained curriculum (see Keeves 1992[2]; Lokan, Ford & Greenwood 1996, 1997). The examination of curricula

(Chapter 2), teaching practices and school resources (Chapter 3) and student learning outcomes (Chapter 4) involves all Australian curricula and data from a Queensland-wide survey of 1467 Year 11 and 12 students, their teachers and schools. Information on these aspects will then provide the basis for an elaborate analysis of the relative impact of the factors on the Economics achievement (Chapter 5). The book concludes with implications for policy- and decision-makers, researchers and educators (Chapter 6).

Chapter 2

The intended Economics curriculum in Australia

An important distinction has been made between the *intended* curriculum, the *implemented* curriculum and the *attained* curriculum (Rosier & Keeves 1991; Lokan, Ford & Greenwood 1996). This distinction assists in the planning, implementation and evaluation of educational policies and practices in that it focuses the attention to different levels of decision making, namely the state or system level, the school or teacher level and the student level.

   The *intended* curriculum is represented in curriculum documents and syllabus statements which provide a rationale as well as aims and objectives for studying a particular subject. In addition, these policy documents outline the content to be taught and the amount of time allocated to the subject, discuss assessment and reporting issues and provide examples of relevant teaching and learning resources. As national or statewide policy documents, they reflect current societal values and priorities.

The *implemented* curriculum is reflected in the resource allocation made to and by schools for the facilitation of the teaching and learning of a particular subject. Moreover, it covers instructional practices such as time allocated to different tasks, selection and design of learning and assessment activities as well as practices of classroom management.

The *attained* curriculum manifests itself in the outcomes of student learning. Indicators of the attained curriculum include measures of achievement in and attitudes towards the subject under consideration.

In Australia, the sovereignty of States regarding primary and secondary education means that each State has the authority to design and implement curricula as it sees fit. However, a national outlook in curricular issues has repeatedly been emphasized in Australia and the

United States (Buckles & Watts 1998; Department of Education Queensland 1991; Hansen 1998; Marsh 1994; Siegried & Meszaros 1997) for pragmatic as well as theoretical reasons. Thus, similarities in curricular content assist student movements across State and Territory borders. Likewise, it facilitates evaluation of applicants' skills and abilities by employers and institutions of further and higher education.

This chapter provides a content analysis of the intended Economics curriculum at the senior secondary school level as the first of the three tiers of curriculum. The purpose of the analysis is twofold.

First, the analysis will result in a measure indicating the level of agreement between the Economics curricula across Australia. Second, the content analysis of the intended curriculum will provide information regarding the opportunity students are given at the system level to learn different economic concepts. This information serves as a background for examining the implemented and attained curriculum as captured in the Economic Literacy Survey - Queensland 1998.

2.1   Design of the content analysis

Content analysis has been defined as "a research technique for the objective, systematic and quantitative description of the manifest content of communication" (Berelson 1952, p. 18). As the aim of the analysis was to arrive at a measure (ie. quantitative description) of the eight curricula in their printed form (ie. the manifest content of communication) the application of this method was considered appropriate.

In terms of the three purposes of content analysis put forward by Holsti (1969), this analysis was designed to compare the content on the same topic (ie. Economics) in two or more texts (ie. Economics curricula of all Australian States and Territories) of the same time period (ie. curricula that were in use in 1998).

Table 2.1:   *Materials in content analysis**

Australian Capital Territory (ACT)	Board of Senior Secondary Studies 1995, Economics course framework education. Australian Capital Territory, Department of Education and Training.
New South Wales (NSW)	Board of Studies New South Wales, 1994 Stage 6 Syllabus. Economics. Board of Studies, NSW, Sydney.
Northern Territory (NT)	same as for South Australia.
Queensland (QLD)	Board of Senior Secondary School Studies, 1992 Senior Economics. Spring Hill, Queensland.
South Australia (SA)	Senior Secondary Assessment Board of South Australia, Economics Stage 1. Extended subject framework. Senior Secondary Assessment Board of South Australia, Economics Stage 2. Detailed syllabus statement.
Tasmania (TAS)	Tasmanian Secondary Assessment Board 1998, Economics. http://www.tassab.tased.edu.au/www/tassab.html
Victoria (VIC)	Board of Studies, 1994, Economics. VCE Study design. Board of Studies, Carlton, Victoria.
Western Australia (WA)	Economics (Year 11) – D304 Economics (Year 12) – E304 http://www.curriculum.wa.edu.au/pages/subj/subj304.htm

Note:

*   *these were the Economics curricula that applied at the time of the study, 1998*

The conduct of the content analysis followed the steps described by Krippendorf (1980, pp. 177-180) and included sampling, data reduction and transformation and analysis.

2.2.1 Sampling

Sampling was not an issue as all manifestations of communication were obtained by securing the written curricula from all States and Territories. Table 2.1 lists the documents that formed the material for the content analysis. All materials were the curricular documents which applied at the time of the conduct of the Economic Literacy Survey in 1998.

First, it is noteworthy that the curriculum of the Australian Capital Territory provided a course framework for Economics. The framework provided a subject rationale but not an overview of economic concepts to be covered in the teaching of the subject.

The Senior Secondary Assessment Board of South Australia provides two curricular documents for Economics, one outlining a program for Year 11 (ie. Stage 1 of the South Australian Certificate of Education, SACE) and one with a program for Year 12 (ie. Stage 2). In Year 11, schools have the option of offering a one-unit program consisting of 50 to 60 hours or a two-unit program which assigns 100 to 120 hours of instructional time to Economics. The Year 11 extended subject framework for Economics specifies five domains:

- environment of business
- roles and processes of business
- communication
- evaluating and responding to change
- social issues and ethics.

The aims include an introduction of fundamental economic principles and their effect upon society, the interaction between economics and the political, legal, environmental, business, ethical, social and cultural aspects of society, and the engendering of an awareness of current economic events. No further details regarding the questions or specific topics to be addressed in order to achieve these aims are provided which creates difficulties for the content coding as it relies to a great extent on the assumptions on the part of the coders as to the specific topics teachers may judge appropriate in the pursuit of the stated aims.

The Year 12 syllabus comprises two units which require a total of 120 hours of programmed school times of which about 96 hours are spent on the study of core topics with the remainder allocated to one optional topic. Here, the issues and questions to be addressed for each topic are more detailed than in the Year 11 document. The South Australian curricula also apply in the Northern Territory.

The Queensland Economics curriculum offers a range of core and elective topics which provides flexibility and choice for students and teachers. The whole course consists of five semester units, each covering a number of topics. The course is designed for a minimum number of 55 hours school time including assessment per semester.

The documentation available from the Tasmanian Secondary Assessment Board encompassed five syllabuses. The most demanding syllabus (*12 EC851 C Economics*), in which some criteria are assessed externally to the school, is designed for a total of 100 hours of class time. One quarter of this is to be spent on each of the four core theory sections with an additional 50 hours of class time allocated to allow students to work on elective projects of their choice. The syllabus *12 EC850 C Economics* encompasses the same content and total of 150 hours of class time but without the external assessment component. Syllabuses *11/12 EC741 B Economics* and *11/12 EC740 B Economics* cover the same number of 100 hours of class time spent on the core theory section but do not contain the 50 hour project component. *EC903 A The Australian Economy* specifies 50 hours of class time in which two of the four theory section topics must be covered. The coding in Table 2.3 (see below) for the Tasmanian curricular material is based on the content specified for the 100 hours class time.

The Victorian Economics curriculum consists of four units whereby Units 1 and 2 are taught in Year 11 while Units 3 and 4 are designed for Year 12. At least 50 hours of instructional time are allocated to each Unit.

The Western Australian syllabus for Economics in Year 11 (*D305*) stipulates 120 hours of class time to cover *The economic framework* as the compulsory section and a choice of three from a set of nine elective sections. The elective sections are:

- the stock market
- the Australian market forms
- economics of labour
- economics of poverty, health and education
- firms and production
- agricultural economics
- environmental economics
- Australian and ASEAN
- minerals and energy economics.

The Year 12 syllabus in Western Australia allocates 110 hours to the teaching of macroeconomics, international economics and government economic policy.

2.2.2 Data reduction and transformation

The structure of the original Test of Economic Literacy (Soper & Walstad, 1987, p. 3-7) provided the framework for coding. The TEL was designed to cover four broad content categories, namely fundamental economic concepts, microeconomic concepts, macroeconomic concepts and international economic concepts. Further details for each of these broad content categories were provided through more specific content categories as listed in Table 2.2.

A team of three experts was used to undertake the content coding. Each curriculum was reviewed by two coders who were instructed to indicate for each document whether each of these 22 content categories was covered...

1.   as a core component of the course (C);
2.   as an elective component of the course (E); or
3.   not at all (N).

Table 2.3 presents the results of the content coding. Each column has two entries, one from each of the two coders. Cells in which the same code is recorded reflect agreement between the two coders in that both either thought that a particular concept was covered in the core (CC), as an elective (EE) or not covered (NN). In contrast, two different codes reflect disagreement between the two coders in their assessment of the content covered. For example, in the Year 11 Economics curriculum for New South Wales, one coder considered competition and market structure to be covered as a core component while the other coder regarded the concept as being covered as an elective. Such disagreement may occur as the interpretation of some of the curricula is not particularly easy.

The last two rows of Table 2.3 summarise the level of agreement between the two coders of each curriculum by providing the number of agreements and disagreements. These two numbers add up to the total of number of concepts (ie. 22) which had to be coded. In order to obtain an estimate of the inter-rater reliability, the coefficient of agreement put forward by Wolf (1997, p. 964) was calculated:

$$\text{Coefficient of agreement or Proportion of agreement} = 1 - \frac{\text{number of disagreements}}{\text{no. of agreements} + \text{no. of disagreements}}$$

While this coefficient does not take into account the proportion of agreement which is expected to occur by chance alone, it was considered appropriate for the purpose of providing an indicator of the level of agreement between coders. When the figures of the two bottom rows in Table 2.3 are inserted into the above formula, coefficients of agreement range from 68 percent in the case of the Year 11 curriculum in the Northern Territory and South Australia to 100 percent for the Year 12 curriculum in Western Australia. The average inter-rater reliability was 82 percent which can be considered to represent substantial agreement between the coders.

Table 2.2:   *Concepts covered in the Test of Economic Literacy*

Fundamental Economic Concepts

1. Scarcity
2. Opportunity cost/trade-offs
3. Productivity
4. Economic systems
5. Economic institutions & incentives
6. Exchange, money & interdependence

Microeconomic Concepts

7. Markets & prices
8. Supply & demand
9. Competition & market structure
10. Income distribution
11. Market failures
12. Role of government

Macroeconomic Concepts

13. Gross national product
14. Aggregate supply
15. Aggregate demand
16. Unemployment
17. Inflation & deflation
18. Monetary policy
19. Fiscal policy

International Economic Concepts

20. Comparative advantage/barriers to trade
21. Balance of payments & exchange rates
22. International growth & stability

Finally, coders were asked to list any concepts mentioned in the curricula that did not appear in the list of 22 categories. This enabled a collation of concepts that might be of specific importance to educators in Australia. The information is presented in Table 2.4.

2.2 Results of the content analysis

The information compiled in Table 2.3 demonstrates the coverage of different economic concepts in two ways: First in absolute terms as to whether or not a particular concept has been covered, and secondly in relative terms which shows the emphasis that one curriculum assigns to a concept in that it is covered either as a core or only as an elective. As mentioned in the above description of the materials, coders were unable to indicate the economic concepts covered in the Australian Capital Territory and had only very general information regarding the topic covered by the Year 11 Economics curriculum in South Australia.

It can be seen that all fundamental economic concepts are covered as core components in the Year 11 curricula of all States and Territories with the exception of Western Australia, where productivity and exchange, money and interdependence as well as economic institutions are not taught as part of the core curriculum. Likewise, all curricula provide coverage of microeconomic concepts in their core sections at Year 11 level.

Concepts pertaining to macroeconomics and international economics are generally covered as core components in Year 12. Only the Tasmanian and Victorian curricula specify the international economic concepts as core aspects in the Year 11 curriculum.
It should be noted that in these two States in particular, curricula intend to expose students to the same core concepts in Year 11 and 12. However, rather than mere repetition, the accompanying notes emphasize that concepts should be covered in greater depth in Year 12. Such spiral curricular coverage which reintroduces the same concepts in order for students to develop a more detailed understanding of the issues and an appreciation of greater complexities and interrelatedness of concepts that previously were treated separately has also been reported for science curricula across the world (Rosier & Keeves 1991).

Table 2.3: TEL concept coverage in Australian curricula

Concepts	ACT	NSW Year 11 12	NT❶ Year 11 12	QLD Year 11 12	SA❶ Year 11 12	TAS❷ Year 11 12	VIC Year 11 12	WA Year 11 12
Fundamental Eco. Concepts								
Scarcity		CC NN	CC CC	CC NN	CC CC	CC CC	CC CC	CC NN
Opportunity cost/trade-offs		CC NN	CC CC	CC NN	CC CC	CC CC	CC CC	CC NN
Productivity		CC CC	CC CC	CC NN	CC CC	NC NC	CC CC	EE NN
Economic systems		CC NN	CC CC	CC NN	CC CC	CC CC	NC NN	NE NN
Institutions & incentives		CC CC	CE CC	CC NN	CE CC	CC CC	CC CN	CN NN
Exchange, money & interdependence		CC NN	CE NC	CE NN	CE NC	CC CC	NN CC	EN NN
Microeconomic Concepts								
Markets & prices		CC NN	CC CC	CC NN	CC CC	CC CC	CC CC	CC NN
Supply & demand		CC NN	CC CC	CC NN	CC CC	CC CC	CC CC	CC NN
Compet. & market structure		CE CE	CC CC	CC EN	CC CC	NC NC	CC CC	EE NN
Income distribution		CE EC	CE EC	CC EN	CE EC	NC NC	CC NC	CC NN
Market failures		CC NN	CC CC	CC NN	CC CC	NC NC	NN CC	CC NN
Role of government		CE CE	CC CC	CC EN	CC CC	CC CC	CC CC	CC NN
Macroeconomic Concepts								
Gross national product		NN CC	NC EC	NN CC	NC EC	NC NC	NN CC	EE CC
Aggregate supply		NN CC	NC CC	NN CC	NC CC	CC CC	NN CC	NN CC
Aggregate demand		NN CC	NC CC	NN CC	NC CC	CC CC	NN CC	NN CC
Unemployment		NN CC	CE CC	NN CC	CE CC	CC CC	CC NC	EE CC
Inflation & deflation		NN CC	CC CC	NN CC	CC CC	NC NC	CC CC	NN CC
Monetary policy		NN CC	CC CC	NN CC	CC CC	CC CC	NN CC	NN CC
Fiscal policy		NN CC	CC CC	NN CC	CC CC	CC CC	NN CC	NN CC
International Econ. Concepts								
Comparative adv./ barriers to trade		NN CC	EE NC	NN CC	EE NC	CC CC	CC CC	NN CC
Balance of payments & exchange rates		CC CC	EE NN	NN CC	EE NN	CC CC	CC CC	NN CC
Int'l growth & stability		NN CC	NN NN	EN CE	NN NN	CC CC	CC CC	NN CC
N coders agreeing		19 19	18 18	20 18	18 18	16 16	21 19	19 22
N coders disagreeing		3 3	4 4	2 4	4 4	6 6	1 3	3 0

(ACT column: details of rationale, goals and assessment given but no indication of topics)

Notes:
❶ Northern Territory follows the same curriculum as South Australia
❷ core concepts covered in Year 11 and 12 are identical except for 11/12 EC903 which only covers two of the four core topics specified in the curriculum
C covered in the core
E covered as an elective
N not covered

28

Table 2.4:   Concepts in Economics curricula not covered in the TEL

Additional Concepts	ACT	NSW Year 11 12	NT❶ Year 11 12	QLD Year 11 12	SA❶ Year 11 12	TAS❷ Year 11 12	VIC Year 11 12	WA Year 11 12
Economic development of Northern Territory	details of rationale, goals and assessment given but no indication of topics	– –	– EE	– –	– –	– –	– –	– –
The firm		CC EC	CE EC	EE –	– –	– –	– –	EE –
History of economic thought		– EE	CC EE	– EE	– –	– –	– –	– –
Economic development and poverty/welfare		– EE	– EE	EE –	– EE	– EE	EE –	EE –
Labour economics		– EE	– –	CC –	– EE	– EE	– –	EE –
Primary industry, agriculture, timber, minerals & energy		– EE	– –	– –	– EE	– EE	CC –	EE –
Income & expenditure analysis		– EE	– –	– EE	– –	– –	– –	EE –
Comparative economic systems		– EE	– –	EE –	– –	– –	– –	– –
Environmental economics		– EE	– –	– EE	– EE	– EE	CC –	EE –
Circular flow		CC –	CC –	CE –	– –	– –	– –	CC –
Stock exchange		– –	– –	EE –	– –	– –	– –	EE –
Tourism		– –	– –	– –	EE –	– –	– –	– –
Personal economics		– –	– –	EE –	– –	– –	– –	– –
Population economics		– –	– –	EE –	– –	– –	– –	– –
Australian and Association of South East Asian Nations (ASEAN)		– –	– –	– –	– –	– –	– –	EE –
Development economics		– –	– –	– –	– EE	– CC	– –	– –
Socialist economies		– –	– –	– –	– –	– EE	– –	– –

Notes:

❶   *Northern Territory follows the same curriculum as South Australia*
❷   *core concepts covered in Year 11 and 12 are identical except for 11/12 EC903 which only covers two of the four core topics specified in the curriculum*
C   *covered in the core*
E   *covered as an elective*
-   *not offered*

In addition to indicating whether or not TEL concepts were covered in the Australian Economics curricula, coders were asked to specify any concepts that were not considered in the TEL but were covered in one or more of the Australian curricula. Table 2.4 provides a summary of these additional concepts.

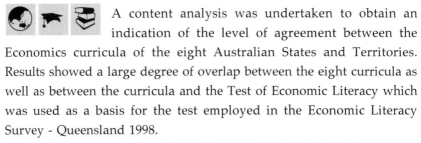 The information presented in Table 2.4 illustrates that a number of concepts which Australian students may opt to study in Year 12 are not covered in the TEL. The concepts include *the firm, history of economic thought, economic development and poverty, income expenditure and analysis, labour economics, comparative economic systems* and *circular flow*. In addition, the coverage of concepts such as *primary industry, minerals and energy* and *environmental economics* reflects the Australian context in which the mining of natural resources is a major economic force.

2.3 Summary

A content analysis was undertaken to obtain an indication of the level of agreement between the Economics curricula of the eight Australian States and Territories. Results showed a large degree of overlap between the eight curricula as well as between the curricula and the Test of Economic Literacy which was used as a basis for the test employed in the Economic Literacy Survey - Queensland 1998.

As school curricula in Australia are within the legislative powers of the States this substantial agreement regarding a core set of economic concepts is of considerable importance. It provides a basis to argue for the feasibility of a national or indeed international assessment of economic literacy. Such a study would be of marked interest given the globalisation of business particularly through recent technological advances like the internet. The speed and immediacy of these interactions require a sound working knowledge of basic economic concepts more than ever before.

It should be borne in mind that some concepts were not covered in the TEL but received coverage in a number of Australian curricula including environmental economics and primary industry, minerals and energy, reflecting the importance of agriculture and mining for the economy of particular States.

Chapter 3

The implemented Economics curriculum

The previous chapter provided an analysis of the Economics curricula across the different States and Territories of Australia. These documents reflect the *intended* curriculum in that they specify the knowledge, skills and abilities students are expected to acquire when undertaking studies in Economics at senior secondary school level.

This and the following chapter describe the way in which these intentions are translated into the *implemented* curriculum by teachers and schools and manifest themselves in the *attained* curriculum as reflected in students' attitudes towards Economics and performance levels in the subject area. The chapters draw on information from a Queensland-wide survey of Economics students in Years 11 and 12, their teachers and school principals as an example of the implemented and attained curriculum in one Australian State in 1998. Before proceeding to the analyses, an overview of the study's aims and objectives, target population, data collection instruments and techniques, and time frame is presented below.

3.1 The study

3.1.1 Aims and objectives

The study, entitled the *Economic Literacy Survey - Queensland 1998*, was preceded by a study in 1997 which was designed to develop and pilot test the validity and reliability of test instruments and background questionnaires. In the absence of an Australia-wide validated economics test, the Test of Economic Literacy (TEL), which had been construct in the United States, served as the basis for the test to assess student levels of economics achievement. In addition, student, teacher and school questionnaires had been developed and pilot tested in 1997 to gather information on student attitudes towards school in general and Economics in particular, teacher background variables such as experience, education and instructional techniques as well as school resources in terms of student/teacher ratio, library resources and equipment available for teaching and learning purposes. As a result of the pilot study (Lietz & Kotte 1997; Kotte & Lietz 1998; Lietz & Kotte 1999), valid and reliable tests and questionnaires were available for the state-wide survey which had the following aims:

- To assess the level of economic literacy of Year 11 and Year 12 students in Queensland;
- To compare the level of student performance in Economics across school types, gender, rural and urban areas;
- To measure perceptions of students, teachers and school principals towards Economics;
- To gain information about the main factors contributing to the development of economic literacy in Queensland;
- To develop estimates of the relative effects of student, teacher and school level factors on Economics achievement;
- To derive policy recommendations for the Queensland school authorities of how to optimize the teaching and learning of basic economic concepts at the secondary school level.

Another major aim of the study was to offer students, teachers and school principals a number of different ways to complete test instruments and background questionnaires, namely by more traditional means in terms of paper & pencil, as well as personal computer and - for the first time in a state-wide survey - the internet.

3.1.2 Target population and achieved sample

In Queensland, Economics is introduced as an elective subject to students only in the upper secondary forms at Year 11 and Year 12. If studying Economics students in Queensland are supposed to elect the subject at the beginning of Year 11 but may only enrol for one year. This explains the generally lower number of students enrolled in Economics at Year 12 compared to Year 11 since a certain proportion decides to drop the subject in the final year of schooling (Bell & Williams 1997).

Education Queensland as the administrative school authority involved was approached in early 1998 to provide the research team with the number of schools offering Economics and the number of students enrolled in this subject. The data made available to the research team originated from a 1997 census and needed to be verified due to some fluctuation expected to have occurred. This was done by contacting each school offering Economics in June 1998 as testing was scheduled for a four-week period in July and August 1998 just before the term break. Schools were asked if and at which year level(s) Economics was taught as an elective. At the same time, information was obtained about the number of students actually enrolled in the first term in 1998.

TARGET POPULATION

All students enrolled at Queensland's State, Independent or Catholic Schools studying Economics at either Year 11 or Year 12 in June 1998.

Of a total of 349 schools in Queensland which had students enrolled at Year 11 and/or Year 12, 222 schools offered Economics. Each of these 222 schools was invited to participate in the survey on a voluntary basis. A sample was not drawn since it was expected that a very sizeable proportion of schools would be interested in joining the project. After the general agreement of the school principal to conduct the survey was reached each school could decide which form of participation it preferred: paper & pencil, PC- or web-based testing.

Table 3.1:   *Desired and achieved sample of Economics students and schools offering Economics at Year 11 and Year 12, by school type (in numbers and percentages)*

Target Population		Schools				Students			
		desired		achieved		desired		achieved	
		N	%	N	%	N	%	N	%
Year 11	State Schools	99	51	30	50	❶	❶	306	35
	Indep. Schools ❷	33	17	20	30	❶	❶	379	43
	Catholic Schools	51	26	13	20	❶	❶	199	22
	total	196	100	63	100	❶	❶	884	100
Year 12	State Schools	102	52	25	48	❶	❶	210	36
	Indep. Schools ❷	30	15	15	29	❶	❶	227	39
	Catholic Schools	50	26	12	23	❶	❶	146	25
	total	195	100	52	100	❶	❶	583	100

Notes:

❶   *no accurate figures could be obtained*

❷   *among the Independent schools are 13 Christian colleges*

Table 3.1 summarizes the desired and achieved sample of students and schools for each of the three school types. Unfortunately, not all schools were willing to provide details about the number of students actually enrolled in Economics. However, the Table shows that nearly one third of all schools teaching Economics decided to participate in the study. As in some schools the Economic Literacy Survey overlapped with general end-of-term - or, in case of the students of Year 12, their final - examinations, not all students from participating schools or classes were able to take the test. However, it can be concluded that around one quarter of the whole target population for each grade level participated in the study.

   Overall, 884 students from Year 11 and 583 students from Year 12 responded to the survey. Even though this is a very satisfactory sample size which is sufficient for a number of statistical analyses it should be kept in mind that the three school types might not be adequately proportionally represented. This affects mainly results that are reported for the different school types as Catholic schools were slightly underrepresented whereas Independent schools were slightly overrepresented in the study.

In order to be able to estimate possible bias due to sampling fluctuation as a consequence of voluntary participation of schools and students attention had to be given to the gender distribution in the Year 11 and Year 12 samples. Table 3.2 presents the distribution of students in the final samples by gender. Studies on Economics from previous years indicated nearly similar enrolment proportions for male and female students (Bell & Williams 1997).

Likewise, recently released school statistics (Bell & Williams 1997; Education Queensland's non-public database information) showed no obvious difference in the enrolment in Economics for schools located in rural or urban areas. However, differences in the enrolment patterns were found with respect to certain school districts.

Based on a classification scheme used by the Australian Bureau of Statistics (ABS 1999) it was possible to calculate the proportion of students attending schools in very rural areas (localities; very sparingly populated), rural areas (shires; countryside, hinterland), so-called statistical local areas (SLAs; smaller rural centers), urban settlements (cities; up to several tens of thousand inhabitants) and metropolitan areas (metro; ie Brisbane).

Table 3.2: *Number and percentages of female and male students studying Economics at Year 11 and Year 12, by school type*

Target Population		Students			
		female		male	
		N	% ❶	N	% ❶
Year 11	State Schools	169	41	115	28
	Indep. Schools	146	36	209	50
	Catholic Schools	93	23	92	22
	total	408	49 ❷	416	51 ❷
Year 12	State Schools	103	39	88	33
	Indep. Schools	85	32	118	44
	Catholic Schools	78	29	62	23
	total	266	50 ❷	268	50 ❷

Notes:

❶ *with the exception of the figure shown for all schools this column shows the proportions of students in the sample for each of the three school types separately for each year level*

❷ *these values show the percentage of female and male students respectively in the sample across all schools in Queensland separately for each year level*

Figure 3.1 illustrates that about half the schools (and students) in the study are located in SLAs, smaller rural centers. This is in accordance with the demographics expected for Queensland when looking at the last Australian census data collected in 1996 (see ABS

Figure 3.1: Proportion of students enrolled in Economics in rural and urban areas for year levels 11 and 12

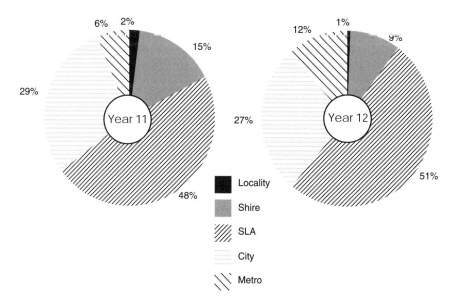

1999). Around one third of all students live in Brisbane, Toowoomba, Cairns, Rockhampton or other cities of the State. Therefore, it is safe to assume that the sample of students participating in the Economic Literacy Survey is not biased with respect to the intake area of the schools.

It should be stated clearly, again, that the two samples achieved for Year 11 and Year 12 Economics students were neither simple random nor cluster samples but rather samples of convenience. However, when comparing the sample characteristics in terms of gender, urban/rural and, to a lesser extent school type, with the relevant information from the Australian Bureau of Statistics and Education Queensland, the achieved sample appears to be reasonably representative.

3.1.3 Data collection instruments and techniques

The Test of Economic Literacy (TEL, Soper & Waldstad 1987) was used as a basis in the development of an instrument to assess students' Economics achievement. As has been shown in the previous chapter, there are different economics concepts covered in the TEL. In order to obtain further information on the validity of the TEL items for use in Queensland context, six Economics teachers had attended a session to rate the appropriateness of the proposed test items for Economics students during the pilot study conducted in Central Queensland in 1997. To streamline this process, the session used a computer based group decision support system facility, called Group Support System (GSS), which generated a summary of the teachers' ratings for each item. This summary, in turn, enabled discussions about items for which ratings differed considerably in order to arrive at a consensus regarding their appropriateness or otherwise. The rating process was undertaken twice, once for each year level.

As a result of this process, 42 items were included in the Year 11 test and 52 items in the Year 12 test. Thirty items were common to the two test forms to allow the equating of student performance. Test items covered the content areas of Fundamental Economic Concepts, Microeconomics, Macroeconomics and International Economics. With few exceptions, students needed less than the maximum amount of 45 minutes to complete the test. Hence, the test was not a speeded but a power test. Reliability and detailed item analyses (Lietz & Kotte, 1999) of the pilot study data provided evidence of the appropriateness of the instrument measuring economics achievement.

In addition to the achievement test, students were asked to complete a Student Background Questionnaire (StBQ). The StBQ was aimed at obtaining information about, for instance, parental education, number of luxury items in the home as an indicator of socio-economic status, the student's learning and leisure habits, or his/her attitudes towards school, different instructional techniques and economic issues.

Figure 3.2:   *Major project steps and time frame of the Economic Literacy Survey*

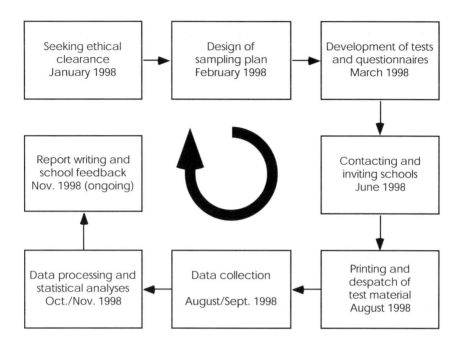

Similar background questionnaires to obtain information from teachers and school principals regarding instructional techniques and educational resources had been designed and pilot tested in the 1997 pilot study. These were used, with minor adaptations, in the 1998 survey.

3.1.4 Time frame

Figure 3.2 illustrates the time frame in which the Economic Literacy Survey was conducted. Development of the study's schedule was mainly guided by the desire to keep the time between data gathering and feedback to schools and the Education Queensland to a minimum as long turnaround times of large-scale surveys have been a major point of criticism (Keeves 1992[1]; Lambin 1995).

This desire was achieved in that only four months passed between the initial contact with schools and the receipt of feedback by schools. Indeed, only seven weeks from the first day of testing to each school receiving a report which specified its achievement levels as well as associated teacher and school characteristics relative to the average achievement across all participating schools.

This extremely short turnaround completed with a minimum of human and financial resources could only be achieved by implementing state-of-the-art data collection methods using PCs and the WWW. An additional advantage of these new data collection techniques was the fact that input from students and schools in remote locations was received at the same time as input from participants in larger cities. This facility of providing real-time, online input was perceived by participants in remote locations to increase significantly the opportunity of having their voices heard.

The following sections present the information obtained from teachers and school principals who participated in the study regarding the way in which they implement the Economics curriculum.

3.2   Teaching practices

Not all teachers of schools participating in the Economic Literacy Survey completed the Teacher Background Questionnaire even though they were given the opportunity to respond by paper & pencil or, alternatively, by using the internet answering the questionnaire online.

 Based on 63 completed questionnaires Table 3.3 shows that a 'typical' high school teacher of Economics in Queensland:

- ■   is between 35 and 44 years of age,
- ■   is permanently employed,
- ■   assigns Economics homework twice a week,
- ■   holds a Bachelors degree,

- rarely or sometimes uses computers in teaching Economics,
- meets other Economics teachers less than once a month, and
- feels sufficiently confident to teach Economics from a newspaper rather than from a textbook.

The teachers in the sample hold Economics specific degrees, most commonly a Bachelor of Economics degree or a Bachelor of Education or Arts with an Economics major or minor. This Economics-specific educational background compares favourably with US teachers who do not major in Economics but rather in subjects like social sciences, history or education (Highsmith, 1990). In terms of gender, an even split emerges with half the Economics teachers being male and half female. This is different to the information about US Economics teachers reported by Highsmith (1990) who ascertained that Economics teachers were typically male.

Queensland teachers, on average, have taught for 14 years in total and ten years in Economics. This compares with a total of 16 years teaching experience and 6.5 years experience teaching Economics in the US data presented by Highsmith (1990). Total teaching experience varies widely, ranging from one to 40 years for total experience and zero to 32 years for teaching Economics. Only half of the respondents have professional experience outside schools, mainly in industry or business and usually for not more than four years.

The majority of respondents teach Economics in both Year 11 and Year 12. Most schools offer five hours of Economics instruction at each year level. Teachers estimate the amount of time it takes a typical student to complete homework to be a bit less than an hour (54 minutes) in Year 11 and a bit more than an hour (67 minutes) in Year 12. However, the standard deviation suggests a considerable range in the amount of Economics homework students are expected to undertake. It is interesting to note that all teachers report spending some time discussing current economic events, with an average of a quarter of lesson time dedicated to this activity.

Table 3.3:   *Overview of teacher variables*

	N	Min	Max	Mean	Std dev	Coding
Personal Characteristics						
Teacher age	63	1	9	4.4	1.9	1- < 25; 2-25-29 3-30-34; 4-35-39 5-40-44; 6-45-49 7-50-54; 8-55-59 9-60 or more
Teacher gender	62	1	2	1.5	0.5	1-female; 2-male
Grade level teaching Economics	61	1	3	2.5	0.7	1-Year 11; 2-Year 12 3-Year 11+12
Employment status	62	1	2	1.0	0.2	1-permanent; 2-contract
Level of study completed in Economics	62	1	6	2.4	1.1	1-none; 2-BA 3-MA; 4-other 5-MA+BA; 6-BA+other
Worked in job other than teaching	62	1	8	1.9	1.5	1-no; 2-industry 3-gov't; 4-oth. 5-ind+gov't; 6-ind+other 7-gov't+oth; 8-all
No. of years outside teaching	31	1	32	6	6	
Years total teaching experience	62	1	40	14	9	
Years teaching Economics	62	0	32	10	7	
Eco. lessons per week Year 11	62	0	10	4	2	
Eco. lessons per week Year 12	62	0	9	4	2	
Meet other Economics teachers	62	1	5	2	1	1-never 2-<once/month 3-once/month 4-once/week 5>once/week
Instruction						
Frequency assigning Economics homework	61	2	5	4	1	1-never 2- < once/week 3-once/week 4-twice/week 5->twice/week
Year 11: average time spent on homework in Economics	56	0	180	54	39	minutes/week
Year 12: average time spent on homework in Economics	57	0	250	67	45	minutes/week

(to be continued)

42

Table 3.3 (ctd.):   Overview of teacher variables

	N	Min	Max	Mean	Std dev	Coding
Instruction (ctd.)						
Use of computers in Economics lessons	61	1	4	2.5	0.8	1-never; 2-rarely 3-sometimes; 4-often
Feeling comfortable to teach from newspapers	62	1	2	1.8	0.4	1 - no; 2-yes
Percent time discussing current economic events	63	5	80	24	17	
Next to textbooks are used...						
...flash cards	62	1	2	1.0	0.2	1-do not use
...hand-outs	62	1	2	1.9	0.3	2-do use
...internet sources	62	1	2	1.8	0.4	
...magazines/journals	62	1	2	1.8	0.4	
...newspaper	62	1	2	2.0	0.2	
...software/comp. programs	62	1	2	1.4	0.5	
...statistics/charts	62	1	2	1.9	0.4	
...videos	62	1	2	1.9	0.4	
Process emphasis:						
Knowledge	62	1	5	3.9	0.9	from
Comprehension	62	2	5	4.3	0.7	1-low emphasis
Application	62	2	5	4.2	0.8	to
Analysis	62	2	5	4.3	0.7	5-high emphasis
Synthesis	62	2	5	4.1	0.8	
Evaluation	62	3	5	4.2	0.7	
Instructional method						
Ability grouping	61	1	4	1.5	0.7	from
Experimental work	61	1	4	1.8	0.9	1-rarely
Group discussion	62	2	5	4.4	0.8	to
Individual study	61	1	5	3.6	1.1	5-frequently
Lecturing	62	1	5	3.3	1.0	
Library work	62	1	5	3.2	1.0	
Small group work	61	1	5	3.3	1.2	
Student investigation	60	1	5	3.8	0.9	
Limitations						
diff.academic ability levels	60	1	3	2.1	0.6	1-not at all
wide range of student backgrounds	60	1	3	1.7	0.6	2-a little bit 3-quite a lot
students with special needs	57	1	3	1.5	0.6	
uninterested students	60	1	3	2.0	0.7	

(to be continued)

Table 3.3 (ctd.):   Overview of teacher variables

	N	Min	Max	Mean	Std dev	Coding
Limitations (ctd.)						
disruptive students	59	1	3	1.7	0.7	1-not at all
parents uninterested in child's learning	60	1	3	1.4	0.6	2-a little bit 3-quite a lot
computer hardware	61	1	3	1.8	0.7	
computer software	60	1	3	1.9	0.7	
other instructional equipment	60	1	3	1.7	0.6	
equipment for use in demos	61	1	3	1.7	0.7	
inadequate teaching facilities	61	1	3	1.5	0.6	
high student/teacher ratio	60	1	3	1.3	0.5	
low morale among teachers	61	1	3	1.4	0.6	
low morale among admins	61	1	3	1.3	0.6	
Content emphasis						
Scarcity	61	2	5	3.9	0.9	from
Opportunity cost	60	1	5	4.0	0.9	1-low emphasis
Productivity	60	2	5	3.7	0.7	to
Economic systems	59	1	5	3.3	1.1	5-high emphasis
Economic institutions	61	2	5	3.1	0.8	
Exchange, money and interdependence	60	2	5	3.4	0.9	
Fundamental Economics	57	2.5	5	3.7	0.6	
Market and prices	61	2	5	4.1	0.7	
Supply and demand	61	2	5	4.4	0.7	
Compet. & market structure	61	2	5	3.6	0.9	
Income distribution	60	1	5	3.3	0.9	
Market failure	60	1	5	3.1	0.9	
Role of government	61	2	5	4.2	0.8	
Microeconomics	60	2.4	4.7	3.7	0.5	
Gross national product	60	2	5	3.8	0.9	
Aggregate supply	60	1	5	3.4	0.9	
Aggregate demand	60	1	5	3.6	1.0	
Inflation and deflation	61	2	5	4.1	0.9	
Monetary policy	60	2	5	4.0	0.8	
Fiscal policy	59	2	5	4.2	0.7	
Macroeconomics	59	2.3	5	3.7	0.6	
Barriers to trade	61	2	5	4.0	1.0	
Bal. of payments/ ex. rates	59	2	5	4.1	0.9	
Int'l growth and stability	59	1	5	3.6	1.0	
International Economics	59	2	5	3.9	0.8	

Newspapers are the most frequently employed teaching material besides textbooks. In addition, teachers use hand-outs, videos, statistics and charts, magazines and journals as well as internet sources as supplementary materials during Economics lessons. Software or computer programs and flash cards, in contrast, are not used for this purpose.

Teachers find that differences in academic ability levels constitute the greatest limitation when teaching Economics, followed by uninterested students. High student/teacher ratios, low morale among administrators or parents who are uninterested in their children's learning are reported not to limit the instructional process.

When asked about the prioritisation of process objectives, Economics teachers assign the highest emphasis to comprehension and analysis whereas only medium emphasis is placed on knowledge. At the same time, teachers use group discussion as an instructional method most frequently, followed by student investigation and individual study. Grouping students according to ability, in contrast, is rarely used. Likewise, experimental work is only sometimes employed, probably because of the limited applicability of this instructional technique to Economics teaching. However, some teachers report that computer assisted activities such as the stock market game, which can be considered to be a quasi-experimental activity, are well received by students. Overall, teachers place highest emphasis on teaching Economics through group-discussions.

Teachers' ratings of the relative emphasis assigned to teaching different content areas reveal that all content receives moderate to high emphasis. In the major content area of Fundamental Economics, opportunity cost receives the highest emphasis while economic institutions are ranked as moderately important. With respect to microeconomic topics, market failure is assigned the lowest emphasis while supply and demand receives the highest emphasis. In the area of Macroeconomics, teachers emphasise fiscal policy the most and aggregate supply the least.

Table 3.4:   *Expected and actual correlations of teacher variables*
                with Economics achievement

Teacher variable	Expected correlation with Economic Literacy	Actual correlation with Economic Literacy
Teaching experience	+	+.04 (ns)
Frequency assigning homework	+	+.23
Time students spend on homework	+	+.27
Perceived limitations in resources	-	-.09 (ns)

Note:

ns   correlation not significant (p>.10)

When teachers' appraisals of these content areas are combined according to major content areas, little differences are found in the mean emphasis on each of the major content areas. This suggests that teachers provide similar coverage of Fundamental Economics, Microeconomics, Macroeconomics and International Economics.

Table 3.4 provides a comparison of theoretical and actual correlations between teacher variables and achievement. The column labelled *Expected correlation with Economic Literacy*, specifies whether a positive or a negative relationship between the listed teacher variables and achievement can be expected as a result of prior research. Thus, students of teachers who have greater teaching experience (Rossmiller 1979; Bodenhausen 1988) more frequently assign homework which takes longer (Anderson et al 1986; Paschal, Weinstein & Walberg 1984) and perceive fewer limitations regarding resources available for teaching (Postlethwaite & Ross 1992) are expected to perform at higher levels.

The right hand column presents correlation coefficients calculated using information from the survey. While the data provide supportive evidence of the direction of the relationship with achievement for all variables under review, only two of the coefficients, namely for the frequency of assigning homework (r=+.23) and the time teachers expect students to spend on homework (r=+.27) reach a notable size.

3.3 The school environment

Table 3.5 reveals some interesting information about the school environment in which the teaching of Economics occurs in Queensland. First, schools differ markedly in size of the student cohort with enrolment figures ranging from 16 students to 2,166 students with an average sized school catering for 800 students. Likewise, numbers of Economics students vary between schools. While in some schools only one student is taking Economics, others had enrolled as many as 119 students in Year 11 and 132 students in Year 12 in 1997. The mean enrolment in Economics per school at Year 11 in 1997 was 17 and 18 at Year 12.

In order to provide for different student numbers, the number of full-time equivalent staff also varies widely. While the smallest school comprises a single teacher, the largest school consists of 220 full-time equivalent teachers. The average number of teachers per school is 55 with slightly more female than male teachers. Approximation of a student-teacher ratio through division of the number of students by the number of teachers reveals an average of one teacher for 14 students. Here, ratios range from as few as eight students per teacher to 29 students per teacher.

The average age of the school principal is between 40 and 44 years with an equal number of male and female principals. The population of the locality in which schools are situated ranges from 868 in regional areas to more than two million in the capital of Queensland, Brisbane.

These population figures were translated into the categories employed by the Australian Bureau of Statistics to obtain an indicator of the degrees of rurality and urbanity in which a school is located. Categories included locality, shire, statistical local area, town, city and metropolitan. Most schools were assigned to a statistical local area (35

Table 3.5:   *Overview of school-level variables*

	N	Min	Max	Mean	Std dev	Coding
Students						
1998 tot. enrol. female students	49	8	1,013	444	236	
1998 total enrol. male students	45	8	1,408	485	312	
1998 total enrolment	53	16	2,166	800	406	
school gender ratio	73	1	2	1.45	.28	1-girls only 2-boys only
1997 female Eco.students Yr 11	44	1	23	9	6	
1997 female Eco.students Yr 12	32	1	34	10	7	
1997 male Eco. students Yr 11	39	1	119	11	20	
1997 male Eco. students Yr 12	30	1	132	14	24	
Total Eco.students Yr 11 - 1997	49	1	119	17	17	
Total Eco. student Yr 12 - 1997	41	1	132	18	21	
Total Eco. students 1997	53	1	251	30	36	
Teachers						
Full-time eq. male teachers	52	0	80	25	16	
Full-time eq. female teachers	53	0	140	31	20	
Total number of teachers	53	1	220	55	34	
Student-teacher ratio	53	8	29	14	3	
Principal						
Age of Principal	52	2	8	5.1	1.7	1- under 25 2-25-29; 3-30-34; 4-35-39; 5-40-44; 6-45-49; 7-50-54; 8-55-59; 9-60+
Sex of school principal	53	1	2	1.5	0.5	1-female 2-male
School context						
Population of locality	74	.868	2,078	86	337	in 1,000
Urbanity-Rurality	74	1	6	3.5	1.2	
School type	74	1	3	1.7	0.8	1-State 2-Catholic 3-Independent

(to be continued)

48

Table 3.5 (ctd.):   Overview   of   school-level   variables

	N	Min	Max	Mean	Std dev	Coding
School resources						
No. of newspaper subscriptions	53	1	6	2.9	1.3	
No. of PCs for students	52	0	1,200	134	170	
No. of PCs for teachers	53	2	1,280	145	179	
internet access	53	1	3	2.9	0.3	1-no 2-staff only 3-yes
Shortage or inadequacy of...						
...heating/cooling/lighting	52	1	3	1.8	0.7	1-not at all
...audio-visual resources for Economics instruction	52	1	3	1.7	0.7	2-a little bit 3-quite a lot
...buildings and grounds	51	1	3	1.6	0.6	
...computer equipment	53	1	3	1.8	0.7	
...library materials for Economics instruction	52	1	3	1.8	0.6	
...instructional materials	51	1	3	1.4	0.6	
...computers for Economics instruction	52	1	3	1.9	0.7	
...instructional space	51	1	3	1.6	0.7	
...specialized ec. staff	52	1	3	1.2	0.5	
...budget for supplies (eg. paper)	52	1	3	1.4	0.6	
...software for Economics instruction	53	1	3	2.2	0.7	
...internet access	53	1	3	1.6	0.7	

schools), followed by city (22 schools) and shires (13 schools). Only one school each was identified as serving a locality and a town respectively and two schools were classified as being located in metropolitan areas. The largest number of schools were State schools (36), followed by Independent schools (22) and Catholic schools (16).

Table 3.5 illustrates that schools subscribe to between one and six different newspapers for the school library, with an average of nearly three per school. While a few schools do not have computers that are available to students, all report computers that are accessible to teachers. However, in most schools some computers are dedicated to the use by staff only but computers set up for students are also available to staff. Nearly all schools report that computers are set up to provide access to the internet for staff as well as students.

Principals are content with the numbers of specialized Economics staff and the available instructional materials. The only areas where principals identified some shortage or inadequacy pertained to software and hardware dedicated to Economics instruction.

As discussed in Chapter 1, evidence on the relationship between school-level variables and student performance in Economics is limited. Nevertheless, the type of relationships between certain school level variables and achievement can be hypothesized on prior research in other subject areas. Thus, Independent (i.e. private) schools (Kotte 1992), schools with fewer perceived limitations in resources (Becker, Greene & Rosen 1990; Madaus, Airasian & Kellaghan 1980) and subscription to newspapers (Postlethwaite & Ross 1992) and schools in urban areas (Kotte 1992) have previously been found to be positively correlated with student achievement. These hypothesized correlations are listed in the middle column of Table 3.6.

 The right hand column of Table 3.6 presents actual correlation coefficients computed from the Queensland survey for these school variables and achievement. The evidence supports the hypotheses in all instances in that high achieving schools are more likely...

- to be located in urban areas
- to be an independent school
- have a lot of students enrolled in Economics and are
- to report no limitations regarding available resources.

Table 3.6:   *Expected and actual correlations of school-level variables with Economics achievement*

School variable	Expected correlation with Economic Literacy❶	Actual correlation with Economic Literacy
School type	Independent (+)	+.35
School is located in an urban area	Urban (+)	+.38
Number of Economics students enrolled in 1997	Larger (+)	+.24 (•)
Number of newspaper subscriptions	More newspapers (+)	+.19 (ns)
Perceived limitations in available resources	Fewer limitations (-)	-.33 (••)

Notes:
❶   *positive correlations with Economics achievement are expected for specified categories .*
ns   *correlation not significant (p>.10)*
•   *number of Economics students enrolled in Year 11 only*
••   *selected variables asking for particular shortcomings at school have been combined into a single factor; a negative sign indicates that the more shortcomings were reported the more likely students were lower achievers in Economics*

3.4   Summary

This chapter has presented information obtained from teachers and school principals in 63 schools regarding the educational context and resources in which Economics is taught in Queensland.

Data showed that the average Economics teacher in Queensland is between 35 and 44 years old, is permanently employed, has 16 years teaching experience in total and six and a half years in teaching Economics, holds a Bachelors degree, meets other Economics teachers less than once a month, assigns homework, rarely or sometimes uses computers when teaching Economics but is sufficiently confident to teach Economics from a newspaper rather than a textbook. Teachers put more emphasis on the concepts of supply and demand, role of government, inflation and deflation, and balance of payments and less emphasis. market failure and economic institutions.

Schools are generally satisfied with their resources, particularly in terms of the Economics specificity of staff qualifications. Nearly all schools have access to the internet but some limitations in the number of PCs available to students and staff is expressed. Likewise, teachers note a shortage of software for Economics instruction.

Correlational analyses between certain teacher and school variables and achievement revealed a number of sizeable coefficients. Thus, frequency of assigning homework and time students are expected to spend on the homework emerged with notable coefficients which indicated that students of teachers who assigned more homework which students are expected to take longer to complete achieved at higher levels in Economics. In addition, analyses revealed sizeable coefficients for the school's location, number of Economics students and perceived limitations in available resources whereby higher performance was recorded for students in urban and larger schools with fewer resource limitations.

However, such bivariate correlations between background variables and achievement are of limited usefulness as other factors may have mediating or moderating effects on the relationship between the two variables. For example, a correlation indicating that urban schools achieve at higher levels then rural schools may disappear once the socio-economic status of the school is taken into account. Or, the quality and quantity of school resources may be mediated by the teachers' instructional techniques to result in higher achievement.

Hence - after a more detailed analysis of achievement levels in Economics overall and in the subdomains of Fundamental Economics, Microeconomics and Macroeconomics in the next chapter - Chapter 5 will put forward an analysis of more complex models of achievement which reflect more accurately the way in which student, teacher and school factors operate to influence achievement.

Chapter 4

The attained Economics curriculum

This chapter reports evidence of the attained curriculum. It provides a profile of students studying Economics in terms of a number of characteristics such as home background, attitudes and leisure activities as well as their levels of performance in this subject. Performance levels are reported in terms of students' total economics scores as well as their subscores in the content areas of Fundamental Economics, Microeconomics, Macroeconomics and International Economics. Scores and subscores are compared along several key characteristics such as gender, socio-economic status as well as type and location of school.

4.1 Student characteristics

This section provides a profile of Economics students in Year 11 and Year 12 in Queensland in terms of age, gender, socio-economic status, leisure activities, other subject choices as well as attitudes to Economics and Economics instruction. The information is derived from the students' responses to questions in the Student Background Questionnaire.

4.1.1 Age and gender

Table 4.1 shows the mean age of Year 11 and 12 students in months, the standard deviation as well as the minimum and maximum values for the overall samples. The mean age for students enrolled at Year 11 is 197 months, or 16 years and five months. This is in line with what was to be expected at the time of testing (July-August 1998).

Table 4.1:   *Age (in months), Year 11 and 12*

	All students Year 11	All students Year 12
MEAN	197	209
STDDEV	6.27	7.28
MIN	178	192
MAX	240	277
N OF STUDENTS	816	523

The mean age for students enrolled at Year 12 is 209 months, equivalent to 17 years and five months. The mean age of the Year 12 students is, therefore, exactly one year above that of the Year 11 students. The fact that the Year 12 standard deviation (7.23 months) exceeds the Year 11 standard deviation (6.3 months) by one month can be explained by students repeating the final year of secondary schooling to obtain higher tertiary entrance scores.

Overall, the age distribution presented for Year 11 and 12 students coincides with the expected age distribution for these year levels. Hence, in terms of age, the sample reflects well the student population at the upper secondary school level in Queensland.

Like age, gender is an important variable when considering the composition of the sample. Of particular interest here is the question whether Economics as an the elective subject is preferred by male or female students. Figure 4.1 comprises a pair of pie charts giving the percentages of male and female students as well as the percentage of students at Year 11 who did not state their gender. Overall the Year 11 sample consist of an even number of male (47%) and female (46%) students with information on gender missing for about seven percent.

The figures for Year 12 students are, in general, similar to those for Year 11 Economics students. No gender differences in enrolment emerge when looking at the overall sample with the male and female

Figure 4.1:   *Proportion of male and female students, Year 11 and 12*

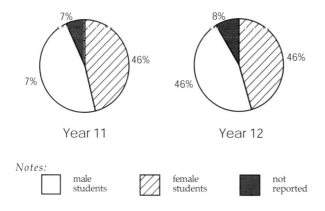

Year 11   Year 12

groups representing 46% of the sample each and eight percent of the students not providing any gender information.

Figure 4.1 illustrates that, overall, Economics appears to be equally attractive to male and female students as an elective at the upper secondary school level in Queensland as demonstrated by the equal proportions of each gender taking the subject.

4.1.2 Socio-economic status of home

Three questions were included in the Student Background Questionnaire to obtain information on three variables as indicators of the socio-economic status (SES) of the student's home, namely...

■   father's educational level
■   mother's educational level and
■   number of books available at home.

These variables have been used successfully in many previous large-scale studies designed to obtain data for the analysis of complex models of school achievement (Carroll 1975; Comber & Keeves 1973; Elley 1992; Postlethwaite & Wiley 1991; Robitaille & Garden 1989).

Tables 4.2 and 4.3 present information about father's and mother's educational level as reported by the Year 11 students for the total sample as well as certain subgroups. Tables 4.4 and 4.5 contain the corresponding information for Year 12 students.

Overall, the educational level of parents is fairly similar for both year groups. While mothers tend to have completed secondary school more often than fathers, the latter appear to have reached a university degree slightly more often than mothers.

Nevertheless, Tables 4.2 to 4.5 reflect sizeable differences when comparing the educational levels of parents across different school types and location. Thus, urban students are more likely than rural students to have parents who completed secondary school or who went to university. Hence, this evidence suggests that the educational level of parents of students attending schools in urban areas is, in general, higher than that of rural students.

When comparing parental education levels according to school type, students in Catholic and Independent schools report higher educational levels for their parents than their counterparts in State schools. This finding is most obviously reflected in the high percentage - often more than a third - of students in Catholic schools who reported university education for their parents. In contrast, only about 10-15 percent of students attending State schools reported their parents to have experienced university education.

Table 4.6 (for Year 11) and Table 4.7 (for Year 12) present information on the number of books found in the students' homes. In general, differences between the grades are marginal. Overall, slightly more than half of all students report to have access of up to 200 books at home.

Table 4.2:   *Father's educational level (in percent); overall sample as well as selected subsamples, Year 11*

YEAR 11

FATHER'S EDUCATION	All students	Female students	Male students	Rural schools	Urban schools	State schools	Catholic schools	Indep. schools
primary	8.4	9.6	8.4	9.6	6.4	13.1	5.0	7.5
secondary	35.2	40.0	35.6	34.0	37.1	39.2	27.7	43.2
vocational	11.2	13.2	10.8	11.7	10.4	10.8	12.1	10.1
university	26.9	24.3	33.2	22.4	33.9	15.0	38.0	24.1
no info	18.3	13.0	12.0	22.3	12.2	21.9	17.2	15.1
N	884	408	416	539	345	306	379	199

Table 4.3:   *Mother's educational level (in percent); overall sample as well as selected subsamples, Year 11*

YEAR 11

MOTHER'S EDUCATION	All students	Female students	Male students	Rural schools	Urban schools	State schools	Catholic schools	Indep. schools
primary	7.2	7.8	7.8	8.0	6.1	9.2	5.3	8.0
secondary	42.2	49.8	49.8	42.1	42.3	50.3	35.1	43.2
vocational	9.0	10.0	10.0	8.7	9.6	6.5	9.2	12.6
university	25.3	22.5	22.5	21.5	31.3	14.1	35.6	23.1
no info	16.2	9.8	9.8	19.7	10.7	19.9	14.8	13.1
N	884	408	416	539	345	306	379	199

Table 4.4: *Father's educational level (in percent); overall sample as well as selected subsamples, Year 12*

YEAR 12

FATHER'S EDUCATION	All students	Female students	Male students	Rural schools	Urban schools	State schools	Catholic schools	Indep. schools
primary	11.3	13.2	11.6	12.7	8.7	15.2	4.0	17.1
secondary	31.9	32.0	37.3	31.3	33.0	34.8	30.8	29.5
vocational	14.1	19.2	11.6	14.1	14.1	16.2	8.4	19.9
university	22.5	19.9	28.7	19.4	28.2	11.9	35.2	17.8
no info	20.2	15.8	10.8	22.5	16.0	21.9	21.6	15.8
N	583	266	268	377	206	210	227	146

Table 4.5: *Mother's educational level (in percent); overall sample as well as selected subsamples, Year 12*

YEAR 12

MOTHER'S EDUCATION	All students	Female students	Male students	Rural schools	Urban schools	State schools	Catholic schools	Indep. schools
primary	11.0	15.8	8.2	10.9	11.2	14.3	6.2	13.7
secondary	40.7	44.0	44.4	41.9	38.3	46.2	33.5	43.8
vocational	12.0	13.5	12.7	9.8	16.0	7.1	15.9	13.0
university	17.8	15.8	22.8	16.2	20.9	11.9	24.7	15.8
no info	18.5	10.9	11.9	21.2	13.6	20.5	19.8	13.7
N	583	266	268	377	206	210	227	146

Table 4.6: *Number of books at home; overall sample as well as selected subsamples, Year 11*

YEAR 11 NUMBER OF BOOKS AT HOME	All students	Female students	Male students	Rural schools	Urban schools	State schools	Catholic schools	Indep. schools
0-10	3.6	3.9	3.8	3.5	3.8	4.9	1.8	5.0
11-25	5.2	5.9	5.3	5.6	4.6	6.9	3.4	6.0
26-100	23.6	27.0	23.8	24.7	22.0	25.8	20.8	25.6
101-200	23.1	26.5	22.8	23.9	21.7	22.9	21.4	26.6
>200	36.5	35.0	43.0	32.5	42.9	30.4	45.4	29.1
no info.	7.9	1.7	1.2	9.8	4.9	9.2	7.1	7.5
N	884	408	416	539	345	306	379	199

Table 4.7: *Number of books at home; overall sample as well as selected subsamples, Year 12*

YEAR 12 NUMBER OF BOOKS AT HOME	All students	Female students	Male students	Rural schools	Urban schools	State schools	Catholic schools	Indep. schools
0-10	3.4	0.4	6.7	3.4	3.4	2.4	3.5	4.8
11-25	6.5	6.4	7.8	7.4	4.9	5.7	4.4	11.0
26-100	20.1	20.3	23.5	19.9	20.4	21.0	19.8	19.2
101-200	20.6	25.2	19.8	19.1	23.3	19.0	22.0	20.5
>200	38.4	44.7	38.8	35.8	43.2	40.5	37.4	37.0
no info.	11.0	3.0	3.4	14.3	4.9	11.4	12.8	7.5
N	583	266	268	377	206	210	227	146

As is the case for parental education, differences emerge between rural and urban students as well as students from different school types. This becomes very visible when taking a look at those groups of students who said they have more than 200 books at home. At Year 12, for example, the difference in this category is more than 10 percent in favour of the urban students.

At the same time, Year 11 students enrolled in Catholic schools much more frequently state to have more than 200 books at home (45.4% at Year 12) in comparison to students from State (30.4%) or Independent schools (29.1%). In contrast, these differences are not found at Year 12.

   It is of concern, however, to find that around five to 15 percent of all students, male and female alike, state to have access to only up to 25 books at home. This small amount of reading material does not seem to offer a sufficient stimulus or base of information. It remains to be seen from results of more detailed analyses if such shortage of reading supplies in the home has an effect on economic literacy when other variables such as parental education or school library resources are taken into account (Chapter 5).

4.1.3 Out-of-school activities

Since time spent in pursuit of leisure activities competes with time available to do homework or to prepare for exams, which, in turn, has been shown to influence achievement (Carroll 1975; Comber & Keeves 1973; Lietz 1996; Postlethwaite & Wiley; Robitaille & Garden, 1989) it is of interest how much time students spend in pursuit of different activities outside school.

Hence, students were first asked to indicate the amount of time spent, typically, during a normal school day on leisure type activities such as...

■   watching television
■   reading for pleasure

- playing computer games and
- doing sports.

Responses are illustrated by stacked bar charts in Figure 4.2 (for Year 11) and Figure 4.3 (for Year 12) showing the time spent on the four types of leisure activities.

Overall, students at Year 11 claim to spend 182 minutes, or about three hours, on such activities with this amount reducing slightly to an average of 172 minutes at Year 12. The reason for this may be connected to the preparation for school-leaving exams in the final school year and an increased choice of leisure time activities (eg. driving lessons, working in a job).

Figure 4.2: *Bar chart of time in minutes per day spent on leisure type activities; overall sample as well as selected subsamples, Year 11*

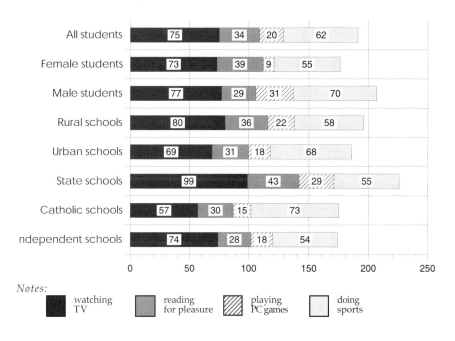

Notes:

watching TV   reading for pleasure   playing PC games   doing sports

61

Figure 4.3: Time in minutes per day spent on leisure type activities; overall sample as well as selected subsamples, Year 12

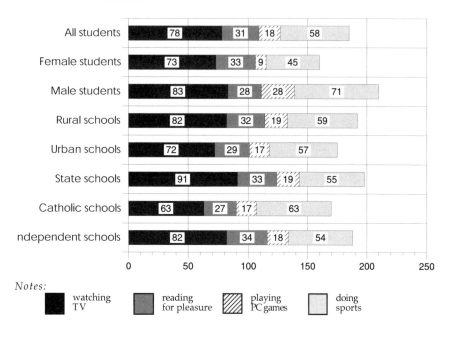

Notes:

| ■ | watching TV | ▨ (grey) | reading for pleasure | ▨ (hatched) | playing PC games | ☐ | doing sports |

Students spend most of their leisure time watching TV (75 minutes at Year 11; 78 minutes at Year 12) and doing sports (62 minutes at Year 11; 58 minutes at Year 12). Combined, these two activities fill nearly 75 percent of the total amount of time spent on leisure type activities at Year 11 and 70% at Year 12.

The results also indicate that male students spend far more time playing computer games and doing sports than female students. Furthermore, students enrolled in State schools report the largest amount of time spent on out-of-school activities, with the largest component occupied watching TV. In contrast, Year 11 students in Catholic schools report to spend nearly one hour less per day on these activities than student in State schools.

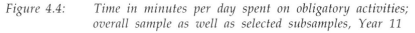

Figure 4.4:   *Time in minutes per day spent on obligatory activities;*
                 overall sample as well as selected subsamples, Year 11

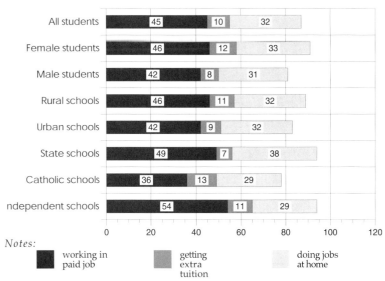

Notes:

■ working in paid job   ▨ getting extra tuition   ▨ doing jobs at home

While the above out-of-school activities reflect the voluntary way to spend one's leisure time, students indicated that part of their time outside school is taken up also by other, more obligatory, commitments such as...

■ working in a paid job
■ getting extra tuition after hours and
■ doing jobs for the family at home.

Figure 4.4 (for Year 11) and Figure 4.5 (for Year 12) present the information on these variables in the form of bar charts for the overall samples as well as for the selected subsamples. It should be noted that the calculations are based on only those students who were engaged in such activities, which were more than 80 percent of all students in the sample.

Figure 4.5: *Time in minutes per day spent on obligatory activities; overall sample as well as selected subsamples, Year 12*

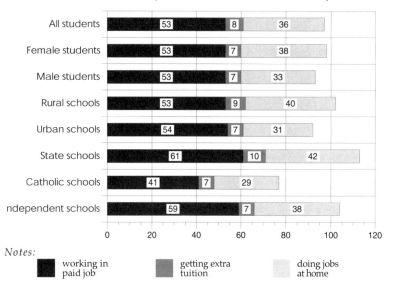

Notes:

◼ working in paid job   ◼ getting extra tuition   ▦ doing jobs at home

Students in Year 11 spend an average of 87 minutes per day on a paid job, extra tuition or home duties which increases to 98 minutes in Year 12 partly because students work more in a paid job. It is interesting to note that Year 11 students from Independent and State schools are much more likely to work in a paid job than students enrolled in Catholic schools. Hence, these duties represent additional demands on time, particularly for students from State and Independent schools who spend nearly two hours per day on such duties. No differences emerge on these variables with respect to gender or location of schools.

The final component of out-of-school activities considered here relates to time spent per day on (a) all homework and (b) Economics homework. Table 4.8 indicates that the largest proportion of students in Year 11 (28.4%) as well as Year 12 (30%) spend up to two hours per day on homework followed by a commitment of up to one hour per day (Year 11=24.8%; Year 12=21%).

Table 4.8:   *Time spent by students on homework (all homework and Economics only), Year 11 and 12*

TIME SPENT ON ALL HOMEWORK PER DAY	% Students Year 11	% Students Year 12	TIME SPENT ON ECONOMICS HOMEWORK PER DAY ❶	% Students Year 11	% Students Year 12
up to 15 minutes	9.9	10.6	up to 10 minutes	20.5	21.6
up to 30 minutes	10.2	14.2	up to 20 minutes	27.0	24.0
up to 1 hour	24.8	21.0	up to 30 minutes	34.8	33.9
up to two hours	28.4	30.0	up to 40 minutes	12.4	12.7
up to three hours	18.8	16.4	> 40 minutes	5.3	7.9
> three hours	7.8	7.8			

Notes:
❶   *on days when Economics homework is given*

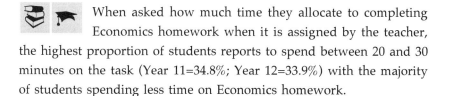 When asked how much time they allocate to completing Economics homework when it is assigned by the teacher, the highest proportion of students reports to spend between 20 and 30 minutes on the task (Year 11=34.8%; Year 12=33.9%) with the majority of students spending less time on Economics homework.

4.1.4   Subject selection by Economics students

Figure 4.6 presents the percentage of Economics students enrolled in other subjects at the upper secondary school level. As students were requested to list all subjects which they were studying, multiple combinations were possible. As a consequence, Figure 4.6 shows percentages of the overall sample of Year 11 and Year 12 students being enrolled in the various subjects rather than absolute numbers.

Due to formal requirements all Economics students take compulsory subjects, which are English and Mathematics. The reason for the percentages in these instances to be below 100 is due to non-response by some students. In addition, more than 60 percent of

Figure 4.6: *Percentage of Economics students enrolled in other subjects*

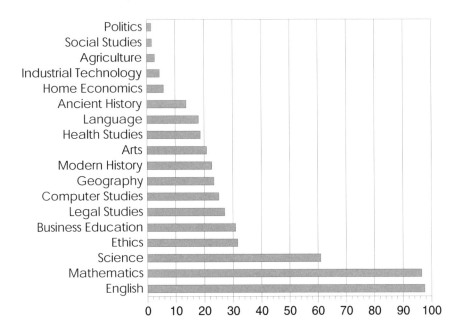

Economics students are enrolled in Science while more than a quarter have chosen Ethics, Business Education, Legal and Computer Studies.

Minor groups of students have decided to study other subjects such as Agriculture, Social Studies and Politics. It is interesting to note that barely any of the Economics students prefer a subject combination with Politics or Social Studies since there should be overlapping curricular aspects. It is likely that, because of this overlap, these subjects are offered in the same time slots in many schools, making them and Economics mutually exclusive (see also Bell & Williams 1997). As a result of competing options for students, it is of interest to ascertain reasons for choosing Economics. Table 4.9 summarises students' responses.

Table 4.9: *Reasons given for choosing Economics as an elective (multiple responses were possible); overall sample*

Reason for having chosen Economics	% students agreeing
It is useful for my future career	56.7
It fits to the other subjects which I study	46.9
I like the subject	45.7
I like the teacher	10.2
I wish to study the same subject as my friends	7.3

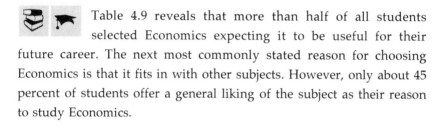 Table 4.9 reveals that more than half of all students selected Economics expecting it to be useful for their future career. The next most commonly stated reason for choosing Economics is that it fits in with other subjects. However, only about 45 percent of students offer a general liking of the subject as their reason to study Economics.

4.1.5 Preferred types of instruction in Economics

In order to enable the more complex analyses (see Chapter 5) to examine whether students preferences for certain instructional techniques had an impact on performance levels, students were also requested to indicate which forms of instruction they preferred in Economics. On a five-point Likert-type scale with the extreme categories of 'very little' and 'very much' students could indicate their liking/disliking for the most common forms of instruction. Table 4.10 shows the mean ratings for the overall sample as well as selected subsamples.

Table 4.10 clearly shows that the mean ratings for each of the types of instruction vary little between the subgroups. Boys and girls, younger and older students, even students from different school types do seem to share the same preferences regarding the various forms of instruction.

Table 4.10: *Preferred form of instruction (mean values indicated by students on a five-point Likert-type scale); overall sample as well as selected subsamples*

PREFERRED FORM OF INSTRUCTION*	All students	Female students	Male students	Year 11 only	Year 12 only	State schools	Catholic schools	Indep. schools
group-discussion	3.88	3.94	3.82	3.90	3.85	3.89	3.83	3.90
small-group work	3.56	3.55	3.57	3.57	3.55	3.55	3.63	3.52
library work	3.30	3.21	3.39	3.31	3.29	3.13	3.25	3.47
experimental work	3.13	3.04	3.22	3.16	3.08	3.14	3.06	3.17
individual study	3.13	3.17	3.08	3.13	3.11	3.02	3.14	3.20
investigation	3.11	3.07	3.16	3.11	3.12	3.13	3.13	3.08
ability-grouping	2.91	2.80	3.02	2.95	2.84	2.91	2.94	2.89
lecturing	2.69	2.67	2.70	2.64	2.76	2.65	2.70	2.70

Note:

* *Likert-type scale; 1="like very little" to 5="like very much"*

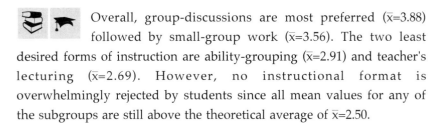 Overall, group-discussions are most preferred ($\bar{x}$=3.88) followed by small-group work ($\bar{x}$=3.56). The two least desired forms of instruction are ability-grouping ($\bar{x}$=2.91) and teacher's lecturing ($\bar{x}$=2.69). However, no instructional format is overwhelmingly rejected by students since all mean values for any of the subgroups are still above the theoretical average of $\bar{x}$=2.50.

4.1.6 Attitudes towards Economics

Another important component of school education is the attitudes (Keeves 1992[1]; Robitaille & Garden 1996) that are developed by students towards school in general and specific subjects in particular. Hence, information regarding student attitudes obtained in the study is also presented in this chapter. The student questionnaire contained a set of 22 Likert-type attitudinal items each to be answered by students on a five-point scale. These items were grouped into two blocks.

The first block comprised seven items for which students were to rate their importance between the extremes 'I think it is not important' to 'I think it is very important'. The second block consisted of 15 attitudinal statements with which students were asked to 'definitely agree' or 'definitely disagree'. Respondents were instructed that there were no right nor wrong answers to these attitudinal questions.

This total set of 22 attitudinal items had been designed as a result of the 1997 pilot study (see Lietz & Kotte 1997; Kotte & Lietz 1998) to provide information on three attitudinal scales, namely *Like Economics* (LIKEECO), *Like school* (LIKESCH) and *Importance of school* (IMPSCH). Results of the factor analysis of the data obtained in the Queensland-wide survey, which confirmed the anticipated three-factor solution, are presented in Table 4.11.

Table 4.11 also provides summary statistics regarding the reliability of each of the scales. Thus, the internal consistency of the scales, expressed as Cronbach's α, amounts to 0.84 in the case of LIKEECO and LIKESCH while that of IMPSCH is only slightly lower with $\alpha=0.72$. These psychometric properties allow for the inclusion of these scales in more complex analyses presented in the next chapter.

In addition, Table 4.11 shows the mean values on each of the three attitudinal scales LIKEECO, LIKESCH and IMPSCH. The mean score for LIKEECO is $\bar{x}=20.69$, thus slightly below the theoretical average of $\bar{x}=21.00$ (ie, the midpoint between the minimum value of 7 and the maximum of 35). This means that the students report an only average liking of a subject which, after all, they have chosen as an elective. Indeed, this result may be rather disappointing for the teachers and the Queensland school authorities as one could expect students who elected a particular subject to display a level of liking which is noticeably above average? Moreover, the relatively large standard deviation of 5.97 provides evidence of quite sizeable differences between students in terms of their liking of Economics.

Table 4.11: *Factor loadings of attitudinal items on three scales; number of items, scale statistics and reliability coefficients; overall sample*

	LIKEECO	LIKESCH	IMPSCH
Economics is important to everyone's life.	0.83	0.10	-0.01
I like Economics.	0.78	0.25	0.08
Economics is useful for my future career.	0.77	0.15	0.10
I would like to continue studying Econ. after school.	0.65	0.08	0.16
Economics should be made compulsory at school.	0.63	0.15	-0.09
I think it is important to do well in Economics.	0.61	0.24	0.41
Economics is an easy subject.	0.54	0.03	-0.01
I really like going to school.	0.12	0.87	0.06
I enjoy being at school.	0.07	0.84	0.07
I find that learning is a lot of fun.	0.24	0.79	0.02
I get satisfaction from the school work I do.	0.27	0.58	0.24
I think it is important to have time for friends.	-0.11	-0.04	0.72
I think it is important to have fun.	-0.10	-0.00	0.71
I think it is important to have money to spend.	0.04	-0.19	0.64
I think it is important to do well in English.	0.12	0.27	0.60
I think it is important to do well at school.	0.22	0.29	0.59
I think it is important to do well in Mathematics.	0.16	0.22	0.48
I can reach a satisfactory standard in my school work.	0.16	0.34	0.45
Number of items in scale	7	4	7
theoretical range of scale	7-35	4-20	7-35
theoretical scale mean	21.00	12.00	21.00
actual scale mean	20.69	12.62	30.31
actual scale stddev	5.97	3.46	3.82
Cronbach's alpha	0.84	0.84	0.72

Students' liking of school in general is expressed by LIKESCH which reaches a mean of x̄=12.62, slightly above the theoretical average of 12 points. But while there is not much more than an average liking of school in general and liking of Economics falls even below (x̄=20.69) what would be expected theoretically (21 points). This finding should give rise to concerns.

Two attitudinal questions were designed to obtain information about future aspects of Economics. Figure 4.7 illustrates the percentage of students for the overall sample and for selected subsamples who expressed their interest to continue studying Economics after finishing school. In addition, Figure 4.8 gives an overview what percentage of students perceive Economics as a useful subject for their future career.

Before interpreting these results further, it should be mentioned here that the vast majority of all students, namely 86 percent, intends to carry on with their studies at university. Another seven percent of the whole sample indicated they wish to proceed to some sort of vocational training while only seven percent of students think that secondary schooling will be the end of their formal education.

 Based on this overwhelming interest to move on to tertiary studies it is somewhat disappointing to find that fewer than four out of ten Economics students foresee a continuation of their economics studies in the future. It is also this number of students who perceive school Economics as being useful for their future career. The question remains why Economics cannot attract more students and why, among those who elected Economics to study at the upper secondary school level, this subject area is insufficiently attractive to be pursued at tertiary level.

When looking at selected subsamples comparing in Figure 4.7 gender, geographic location or school type these general findings hardly vary. On the whole, Economics is rather not the subject to study after school and, consequently, Economics - even for specific subgroups - is principally not important for the future career.

Figure 4.7: *Percent of students wishing to continue studying Economics after school; overall sample and selected subsamples*

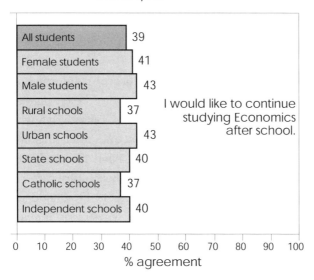

Figure 4.8: *Students (in %) considering Economics useful for their future career; overall sample and selected subsamples*

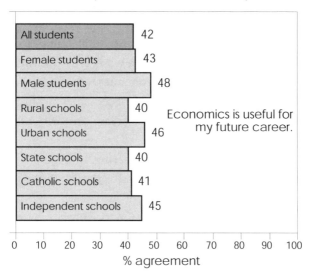

Figure 4.9: *Percent of students considering school and selected subjects as being important;*

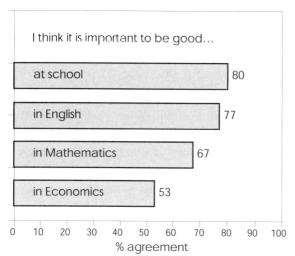

I think it is important to be good...

at school	80
in English	77
in Mathematics	67
in Economics	53

% agreement

Thus, less than half of the student seem to find the study of Economics beneficial. One might be tempted to assume that students at the end of secondary schooling may feel some sort of saturation with school in general and, thus, do not attribute much importance to any school subject.

However, Figure 4.9 clearly demonstrates that this is not the case. The expressed attitude is Economics-specific as it is different for Mathematics, English or school per se. It should be reemphasized that these findings reflect the attitudes of students who have elected to enrol in Economics.

Against this background of student characteristics, the remainder of the chapter presents information regarding the performance levels in Economics to complete the profile of Economics students at the upper secondary school level.

4.2 Performance levels in Economics

Performance in Economics was measured using the Australian adaptation of the Test of Economic Literacy (TEL, Soper & Walstad, 1987). Test items covered the content areas of Fundamental Concepts, Microeconomics, Macroeconomics and International Economics (see Chapter 3).

Scores were calculated for each student for the overall test as well as the four major content areas. Rather than reporting performance in terms of raw scores or percentage values, it was decided to calculate Rasch scores as performance indicators. The Rasch model (Rasch, 1960) is defined in terms of probabilities whereby the probability of a person answering an item correctly is related to the person's level of ability on the latent trait being measured, relative to the difficulty level of the item. In other words, a person is able to obtain a higher score even if he or she has answered fewer items than another person provided that the items answered are of greater difficulty. The Rasch model calculates levels of item difficulty relative to all other items. At the same time, persons' ability levels are calculated relative to the ability levels of all other test-takers. As a consequence, Rasch scores have been used in a number of recent large-scale educational surveys as the preferred means of performance measure (Elley 1992; Martin & Kelley 1996; Keeves 1992[1]). One of the key benefits is the fact that Rasch scores can be used readily to compare achievement gains across year levels. The software package QUEST which was used in this study to calculate Rasch scores was developed by Adams and Khoo (1993).

4.2.1 Economic literacy levels at Year 11

Scores for Year 11 students were based on the 42 test items of which 13 were assigned to the Fundamental Concepts subscale, 12 to the Microeconomics subscale and 14 to the Macroeconomics subscale.

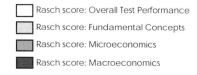

Four separate Rasch scores have been calculated, namely for the Overall Test Performance as well as for the subsets of items assessing Fundamental Concepts, Microeconomics and Macroeconomics. Different grey shadings facilitate the distinction between these scores (see Figure 4.10).

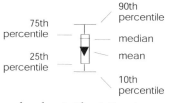

A common format to display test performance graphically are so-called box plots. In addition to the mean score, box plots display the median, the 10th, 25th, 75th and 90th percentile within each school. The following symbols are used (see Figure 4.10).

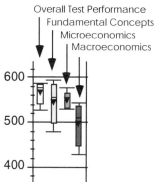

The four Rasch scores have been plotted next to each other in order to assist with the comparison of performance levels.

As in previous studies (Elley 1994; Lokan, Ford & Greenwood 1996, 1997; Keeves & Kotte 1996; Lietz 1996), Rasch scores are reported on a scale ranging from 0 to 1000 with 500 as the mean.

Figure 4.10 consists of six panels. In each panel, four box plots are shown, one for the total scale and one for each of the three subscales, namely Fundamental Concepts, Microeconomics and Macroeconomics. The first panel on the left illustrates the performance of all Year 11 students in Queensland. The next two panels provide the box plots for female and male students. The last three panels on the right show performance levels for the three different school types.

Figure 4.10 illustrates that Year 11 students achieve the highest level of competence in Macroeconomics which covers concepts such as gross national product, inflation and deflation as well as monetary and

Figure 4.10: *Economic Literacy Levels expressed in Rasch scores for the overall sample (N=884) as well as for selected subsamples, Year 11*

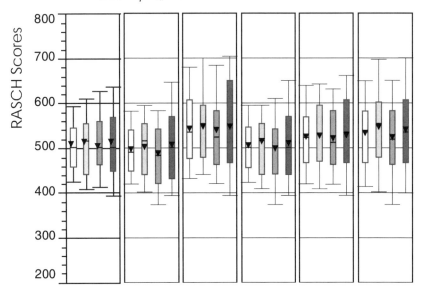

fiscal policy. In contrast, students show the lowest performance level in Microeconomics in which concepts such as markets and prices, supply and demand as well as competition and market structure are discussed. An examination of the variation of scores reveals a considerably greater range of performance levels between students on the Macroeconomics subscale than on the Microeconomics subscale - an observation which holds for all types of schooling.

Figure 4.10 and the corresponding information in Table 4.12 clearly show gender differences between the performance of male and female students. Thus, scores on the total scale as well as all subscales are considerably higher for male students than for female students. At the same time, Figure 4.10 illustrates that the range of achievement levels between the highest and the lowest achievers is greater for boys than it is for girls. On the Macroeconomics

Table 4.12: *Rasch scores and standard deviations (in brackets) for the overall sample as well as for selected subsamples, Year 11*

	All QLD (N=884)	All Females (N=408)	All Males (N=416)	State Schools (N=306)	Indep. Schools (N=379)	Catholic Schools (N=199)
ALL TEST ITEMS	521 (86)	511 (72)	532 (96)	500 (73)	542 (89)	515 (88)
FUNDAMENTAL CONCEPTS	527 (102)	517 (93)	539 (109)	508 (89)	547 (111)	518 (97)
MICROECONOMICS	514 (104)	500 (93)	529 (114)	492 (88)	537 (107)	506 (112)
MACROECONOMICS	529 (115)	523 (102)	536 (127)	506 (105)	549 (116)	528 (122)

subscale, for example, the lowest performing boys are as low performing as the lowest female performers. Yet, 75 percent of boys achieve at a level at which only the highest female performers can be found in Macroeconomics.

A t-test of the mean differences demonstrates that all differences would be significant, except for the Macroeconomics subscale, if the data stemmed from a simple random sample. However, as in most educational research, the sample in this study was not a simple random sample. Rather, participation was voluntary and intact classes were tested within schools. Hence, it is more appropriate to use the significance test as an indicator of noteworthy gender differences in Economics achievement.

While gender differences in Economics achievement have been reported in some studies (Walstad & Robson 1997), no significant differences between male and female students had emerged in the 1997 pilot study at the total score, subscore or item levels (Kotte & Lietz 1999). Moreover gender differences have frequently been shown to be mediated by other factors such as homework effort or type and extent of out-of-school activities (Keeves 1992[1]; Kotte 1992). Hence, it will be of interest to look beyond a bivariate relationship between gender and achievement and examine the emerging gender differences in a larger model of factors influencing Economics performance (see Chapter 5).

  Figure 4.10 also reveals differences between achievement levels of different school types. Thus, students enrolled in Independent Schools show the highest level of performance across all scales, followed by Catholic and State Schools. State Schools exhibit the lowest spread of scores for the total scale and the subscale measuring Fundamental Concepts in Economics. In contrast, the spread of scores for the Fundamental Economics subscale displayed for Catholic Schools is considerable. Here the lowest achievers perform below the lowest performers in State Schools while the upper 25 percentile of students in Catholic Schools achieves at a higher level than the highest achievers in the State Schools on the Fundamental Economics subscale.

For the Microeconomics subscale, Independent Schools show a lower range of ability levels than State Schools while the range reported for Macroeconomics is similar for the two school types. Again, Figure 4.10 illustrates that the differences between high achieving and low achieving students is greater in Catholic Schools than in State or Independent Schools.

It should be noted, though, that such comparisons of mean performance levels - as already pointed out above for the gender differences - are frequently misleading in that they fail to consider important variables that lead to these differences in achievement. With respect to school types, for example, it is frequently argued (Postlethwaite & Wiley 1991; Kotte 1992; Keeves 1996) that not the school type by itself but the associated differences in resource levels contribute to differences in student performance. Hence, it will be again of interest to incorporate these variables in a more sophisticated model of factors influencing Economics achievement to estimate the effects of different variables on achievement while holding the effects of other important variables constant (see Chapter 5).

4.2.2 *Economic literacy levels at Year 12*

The Year 12 test comprised 52 items of which 14 were assigned to the Fundamental Concepts subscale, 15 to the Microeconomics subscale, 13 to the Macroeconomics subscale and 10 to the subscale measuring International Economics. The latter scale was only added at Year 12 level as a teacher rating of the test items in the Central Queensland Pilot Study in 1997 had shown that the content required to answer these items was not taught until Year 12.

Hence, five Rasch scores were calculated for this year level, namely for the Overall Test Performance as well as for the subsets of items for Fundamental Concepts, Microeconomics, Macroeconomics and International Economics. Different grey shadings facilitate the differentiation between these scores (see also Figure 4.11).

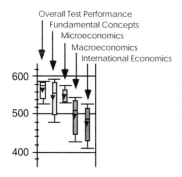

Again, box plots of Rasch scores were created for the total as well as for the subscales. Figure 4.2 shows these box plots for the overall test performance of all Year 12 students in Queensland, as well as subgroups such as female and male students as well as the three different school types. In addition to the total score, performance levels for the total sample as well as the subgroups are reported for the subscales of

Figure 4.11:   *Economic Literacy Levels expressed for the overall sample (N=583) as well as for selected subsamples, Year 12*

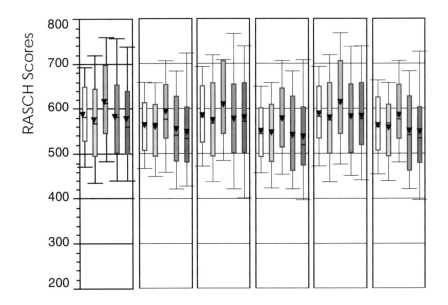

Fundamental Concepts, Microeconomics, Macroeconomics and International Economics (see also Figure 4.11).

Figure 4.11 shows that Year 12 students achieve the highest level of competence in Microeconomics. This is in contrast to the findings for Year 11 students who exhibited the lowest performance on that subscale. This is likely to reflect the shift in the content focus from Year 11 to Year 12. The high performance in Microeconomics (594) is followed by the mean achievement on the Fundamental Concepts subscale (562), which is closely followed by the mean score for Macroeconomics (559) and International Economics (558). Like the Year 11 data, Year 12 results show that differences between the highest and lowest achievers is greatest for the Macroeconomics subscale.

The scores presented in Figure 4.11 and Table 4.13 are consistently higher for male than for female students across the total as well as the

Table 4.13:   *Rasch scores and their standard deviations (in brackets) for the overall sample as well as for selected subsamples, Year 12*

	All QLD (N=583)	All Females (N=266)	All Males (N=268)	State Schools (N=210)	Indep. Schools (N=227)	Catholic Schools (N=146)
ALL TEST ITEMS	568 (86)	560 (76)	578 (95)	550 (79)	589 (92)	562 (81)
FUNDAMENTAL CONCEPTS	562 (103)	556 (91)	567 (114)	546 (98)	580 (114)	557 (88)
MICROECONOMICS	594 (101)	590 (97)	603 (105)	577 (92)	615 (111)	585 (91)
MACROECONOMICS	559 (117)	551 (108)	569 (125)	541 (111)	583 (115)	549 (121)
INTERNATIONAL ECONOMICS	558 (124)	544 (110)	574 (135)	538 (118)	583 (126)	548 (125)

four subscales. A t-test of the mean achievement levels reveals that these differences are only significant for the total and the International Economics subscore. As above, this test should only be regarded as a guide. As is the case for Year 11, girls are a more homogeneous group with regard to their performance in that the difference between the highest and lowest achievers among boys is greater than for girls.

A finding at the Year 11 level which also emerges in the Year 12 data is that students from Independent schools show the highest performance across all scales, followed by students from Catholic and State schools. At the same time, an examination of the spread of scores reveals the greatest differences between high and low achievers for Independent schools. Only for the International Economics subscale are differences between the highest and lowest achievers greatest in Catholic schools.

In summary, all students at Year 12 perform well above average (568). However, noticeable and partially significant differences are found when comparing Independent, Catholic and State schools. Though this is not necessarily surprising - and in line with findings relevant for other subjects at the upper secondary school level (Lokan, Ford & Greenwood 1996, 1997) - students enrolled in Independent schools perform, on average, better than other students.

4.2.3 Economics achievement and means of data collection

One key element of the Economic Literacy Survey was the attempt to explore new ways of school assessment and data collection introducing the possibilities of PC- and WWW-based test administration.

The PC and WWW tests had been designed with the intention to preserve the greatest possible similarity in format and 'handling'. Both new options, for example, allowed students during the test administration to scroll forward and backward at their own pace and liking, much the same as if they turn a page forward or backward. Corrections to answers made were also possible at any time. Only the instructions to students how to proceed with testing were different. Regardless of the test option students were supervised by their Economics teacher.

It was of particular concern to investigate whether the three subgroups performed equally well or if the format of testing did, perhaps, influence the outcome. Tables 4.14 (for Year 11) and 4.15 (for Year 12) illustrate how the three subgroups scored in the overall test as well as in the three subdomains.

When asked to choose the PC or WWW for testing several schools stated technical and administrative difficulties since often PC installations at school were booked out at the time of testing or insufficient numbers of useable PCs were available. Economics

Table 4.14:   Rasch scores Year 11 (standard deviations in brackets),
number of students and number of schools tested via
paper & pencil, PC and World Wide Web

	Paper & Pencil	Personal Computer	World Wide Web
ALL TEST ITEMS	526 (86)	491 (93)	518 (76)
FUNDAMENTAL CONCEPTS	536 (101)	482 (104)	520 (98)
MICROECONOMICS	521 (106)	480 (111)	507 (90)
MACROECONOMICS	530 (115)	511 (128)	534 (109)
N OF STUDENTS PARTICIPATING	630	89	164
N OF SCHOOLS PARTICIPATING	42	8	16

Table 4.15:   Rasch scores Year 12 (standard deviations in brackets),
number of students and number of schools tested via
paper & pencil, PC and World Wide Web

	Paper & Pencil	Personal Computer	World Wide Web
ALL TEST ITEMS	565 (91)	578 (65)	573 (78)
FUNDAMENTAL CONCEPTS	558 (105)	559 (98)	573 (99)
MICROECONOMICS	592 (104)	613 (88)	593 (96)
MACROECONOMICS	560 (124)	563 (86)	558 (106)
INTERNATIONAL ECONOMICS	548 (124)	593 (121)	573 (124)
N OF STUDENTS PARTICIPATING	390	45	148
N OF SCHOOLS PARTICIPATING	28	7	17

teachers, who were meant to administer the test at their school site,
were hesitant to try the PC option since they anticipated hard- or
software related difficulties. In contrast, schools which opted to conduct
the survey on the internet reported, in general, no major problems or
technical obstacles.

While, on the surface, the scores of the students taking the test using the 'traditional' paper & pencil approach seemed to trail behind those of the other subsamples this may be partly the result of unbalanced sample sizes. It is, however, encouraging to learn that when performing t-tests between the subgroups, in general, no significant differences emerged between the three formats of assessing economic literacy among Year 12 students (see Table 4.15). Even at Year 11, no differences were found between the subgroups of paper & pencil and WWW (Table 4.14).

 These findings support a general shift to move towards the use of PC- and internet-based testing, where this is pedagogically appropriate and technically feasible.

4.2.4 Economics achievement in rural and urban areas

Since the Economic Literacy Survey included data collected in schools throughout the State it is of particular interest to see if performance differences are found in Economics that can be attributed to the location of the school. Commonly, school performance was regarded as being lower in rural areas compared to schools located in urban or metropolitan areas: students being enrolled in rural schools are believed to be disadvantaged (Lokan, Ford & Greenwood 1996, 1997).

Initially, it was recorded for each school in which of the following type of locations it was situated. This classification was derived from the 1996 census conducted by the Australian Bureau of Statistics. The following six demographic categories were coded (ABS 1996):

1. Locality
2. Shire
3. Statistical Local Area
4. Town
5. City
6. Metropolitan Area

Table 4.16: Rasch scores (standard deviations in brackets) for Year 11 students enrolled in rural and urban schools as well as differences between them; number of students and significance level based on t-test means comparison

	students in rural areas	students in urban areas	difference (urban-rural)	sign. level
ALL TEST ITEMS	509 (79)	540 (92)	31	.0000
FUNDAMENTAL CONCEPTS	515 (96)	545 (108)	30	.0000
MICROECONOMICS	496 (96)	543 (110)	47	.0000
MACROECONOMICS	521 (111)	541 (121)	20	.0099
N OF STUDENTS IN SUBGROUP	539	345		
PERCENTAGE OF STUDENTS IN SUBGROUP	61	39		

In order to clarify possible differences arising from their location, schools were then ascribed the index 'rural' if they fell in the categories 'locality', 'shire' or 'Statistical Local Area'. Likewise, schools located in 'urban' areas came from towns, cities or metropolitan Brisbane. Using this classification there were about 60 percent of students enrolled in rural and 40 percent in urban schools.

Table 4.16 illustrates the performance differences with respect to economic literacy in favour of Year 11 students who come from urban areas. In fact, the overall difference recorded of 31 Rasch points is considerably higher than the differences found between male and female students or between the various types of schools. Indeed, given previous estimates (Keeves 1992[1]) this difference is approximately equivalent to a year of schooling.

As can be seen from the t-test results, the mean differences between students from rural and urban areas at Year 11 are rather strong. The differences are highly significant for the overall performance as well as for each of the subscores, the highest difference being recorded for Microeconomics (47). Since the performance differences at this year level between rural and urban students in the

Table 4.17: *Rasch scores (standard deviations in brackets) for Year 12 students enrolled in rural and urban schools as well as differences between them; number of students and significance level based on t-test means comparison*

	students in rural areas	students in urban areas	difference (urban-rural)	sign. level
ALL TEST ITEMS	555 (82)	592 (90)	37	.0000
FUNDAMENTAL CONCEPTS	548 (100)	588 (105)	40	.0000
MICROECONOMICS	581 (98)	616 (102)	35	.0001
MACROECONOMICS	544 (112)	588 (119)	44	.0000
INTERNATIONAL ECONOMICS	543 (120)	585 (127)	42	.0001
N OF STUDENTS IN SUBGROUP	377	206		
PERCENTAGE OF STUDENTS IN SUBGROUP	65	35		

other subject areas are much smaller it can be inferred that rural schools might resort to putting different emphasis on what is actually taught at Year 11 with Microeconomics being neglected.

The greater variance in the performance of urban students compared to their rural counterparts should also be mentioned with the greatest standard deviations recorded for the subdomain of Macroeconomics.

Similar findings are obtained for students at Year 12. As Table 4.17 shows, the overall differences between rural and urban students are even higher in Year 12 than in Year 11. The gaps found with respect to performance between the two subgroups of students are consistent across the four content areas, most noticeable in Macroeconomics (44).

The results presented in Tables 4.16 and 4.17 indicate that attention has to be paid to investigate further the effects contributing to the quite sizeable differences recorded between the achievement of students attending school in rural or in urban areas.

4.2.5 Change in achievement from Year 11 to Year 12

For the purpose of estimating the change in achievement from Year 11 to Year 12, 30 common items were included in the two tests. This allowed for a Rasch analysis to be undertaken to equate the performance between the two year levels. In this context, it is important to differentiate between two stages in the Rasch analysis, namely calibration and scoring (see also Keeves & Kotte 1996 for further statistical discussion). Calibration refers to the calculation of item difficulty levels or thresholds while scoring denotes the estimation of scores taking into account the difficulty levels of the items answered by a student.

The following steps were undertaken to equate the Year 11 and Year 12 scores. First, a Rasch analysis was performed using the responses of only those Year 11 students who had attempted all items (N=298). The use of only those students was intended to minimize the potential of bias introduced as a result of the inappropriate handling or ignoring of missing data as a result of differences in student test-taking behaviour or differences in actual testing conditions. Year 11 item threshold values for those 30 items that were common to the Year 11 and Year 12 test are recorded in Table 4.18.

Likewise, a Rasch analysis was performed using the responses of only those Year 12 students who had attempted all items (N=494) and the resulting threshold values for those 30 items that were common to the Year 11 and Year 12 test were recorded in Table 4.18. An examination of the Year 11 and Year 12 item threshold values reveals that the common items are easier for the Year 12 students.

Differences were calculated between the Year 11 and Year 12 threshold values of common items and the sum of all differences was divided by the number of common items (ie. 30). The resulting mean difference was 0.25 points.

In the next step, all 42 items of the Year 11 test were calibrated using students who had answered all items (N=494) and the resulting item threshold values were used as anchor values during scoring.

Table 4.18:   *Rasch estimates of item thresholds for 30 items common to Year 11 and Year 12*

Common Item No.	Item Thresholds Year 12 (N=298*)	Item Thresholds Year 11 (N=494*)	Difference Year 12 -Year 11
1	-1.33	-1.54	0.21
2	-1.38	-1.53	0.15
3	-0.94	-1.32	0.38
4	-1.13	-1.28	0.15
5	-1.18	-1.35	0.17
6	-1.65	-1.83	0.18
7	-0.48	-0.73	0.25
8	-0.11	-0.29	0.18
9	0.26	-0.12	0.38
10	0.43	0.14	0.29
11	-0.28	-0.46	0.18
12	-0.10	-0.41	0.31
13	-1.17	-1.16	0.01
14	0.53	0.58	0.05
15	0.63	0.61	0.02
16	0.27	-0.14	0.41
17	-0.40	0.06	0.46
18	-0.01	0.00	0.01
19	0.62	0.55	0.07
20	0.62	0.40	0.22
21	-0.43	-0.77	0.34
22	0.83	0.61	0.22
23	0.47	0.57	0.10
24	0.54	0.23	0.31
25	1.58	1.42	0.16
26	1.55	1.11	0.44
27	1.58	1.12	0.46
28	1.05	0.60	0.45
29	0.52	0.83	0.31
30	2.79	2.13	0.66
		Total difference	7.53
		Average difference (=7.53/30)	0.25

Note:

*   *only students answering all items were used during calibration*

Table 4.19:   Equating of Economics performance - Year 11 and 12

Year 12 mean total Rasch score (N of students=583; n of items=52)	568
Year 11 mean total Rasch score (N of students 884; n of items=42)	521
Raw difference (Year 12 - Year 11)	47
Gain from Yr 11 to Year 12, adjusted for growth (ie. 0.25)	22

Then, Rasch scores were calculated for all students at Year 11 (N=884) using all items (n=42) ignoring any items that students had omitted or not reached. The resulting average (521) was used for equating.

The same steps were followed for the equating process for the Year 12 data. Thus, calibration was undertaken using only students who had answered all 52 items. The resulting item thresholds were used as anchor values during scoring of responses by all 583 Year 12 students. The resulting mean score (568) was used for equating.

As the final step, in order to undertake the actual equating, the mean Rasch score for the Year 11 students (521) was subtracted from the mean Rasch score for the Year 12 students (568). This raw difference of 47 points was adjusted for the expected higher performance of Year 12 students by subtracting the mean difference of 26 points. Thus, the gain from Year 11 to Year 12 was calculated to be 22 Rasch scale points. Table 4.19 illustrates this calculation.

Keeves (1992[1], p. 8) states that an increase of 33 score points equates to one year of schooling. Hence, the resulting gain score of 22 Rasch score points is equivalent to approximately two thirds of a year of schooling.

4.3 Correlations of student characteristics with achievement

As is the case for teacher and school variables (see Chapter 3), findings of previous research studies allow a number of hypotheses to be developed regarding the correlation between certain student characteristics and achievement.

The middle column of Table 4.20 presents these hypothesized correlations. Thus, for example, male students are expected to outperform female students in Economics (Gleason & Van Scyoc 1995; Walstad & Soper 1987). Likewise, students with more highly educated parents and more books in the home have previously demonstrated higher levels of performance (Husén 1967; Lehmann et al 1995; OECD 1998; Purves 1992; Thorndike 1975; Wagemaker 1993). Furthermore, current performance levels have been shown to be highly associated with aptitude as reflected in students' prior performance has been demonstrated by Keeves (1972), Kotte (1992), Lietz (1996) and Lietz and Kotte (1998). Finally, strong relationships have been reported between achievement and (a) student attitudes towards school in general and individual subjects in particular (Keeves & Kotte 1995; Kotte 1992), (b) time spent on different out-of-school activities such as homework, sport and TV watching (Binkley & Rust 1994; OECD 1998; Wagemaker 1993), and (c) educational aspirations (Elley 1992; Lehmann et al 1995; Lietz 1992).

The right hand column in Table 4.20 lists the correlation coefficients for each of the student level variables with achievement in Economics. Overall, the actual correlations coincide with the hypothesized relationships. Thus, correlation coefficients indicate higher achievement for teenagers of mothers (0.13) and fathers (0.17) who have completed higher levels of education, who spend less time watching TV (-0.12), doing sports (-0.10) or working for money (-0.10) or at home (-0.10), who have more positive attitudes to Economics (0.20) and who expect to proceed to tertiary education.

Table 4.20: Expected and actual correlations of student-level variables with Economics achievement

Student variable	Expected correlation with Economic Literacy	Actual correlation with Economic Literacy
age of student	+	0.00 (ns)
student's gender	+•	0.12
father's educational level	+	0.17
mother's educational level	+	0.13
no. of books at home	+	0.20
last year's result in English	+	0.31
last year's result in Mathematics	+	0.26
time spent on all homework	+	0.08
time spent on Economics homework	+	-0.02 (ns)
hrs watching TV	-	-0.12
hrs doing sports	-	-0.10
hrs working in paid job	-	-0.10
hrs doing jobs at home	-	-0.10
IMPSCH••	+	0.06
LIKESCH••	+	0.03 (ns)
LIKEECO••	+	0.20
expected educational level	+	0.21

Notes:

ns   correlation not significant (p>.10)

•   positive correlation indicating a higher performance of boys, who are coded '2' compared with girls who are coded '1'

••   items asking for students' levels of agreement with particular statements were combined through factor analysis into attitudinal scales (see Table 4.11)

The absence of an expected positive correlation between achievement and age may be evidence of the fact that the developmental advantage of older students is counteracted by the fact that considerably older students are usually repeaters and, hence, lower achievers. The negative correlation between time spent on Economics homework and achievement is also unexpected. However, the size of the coefficient is too small to suggest that doing more Economics homework is associated with lower achievement.

4.4   Summary

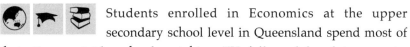 Students enrolled in Economics at the upper secondary school level in Queensland spend most of their time outside school watching TV followed by doing sports, working at a paid job and doing chores around the home. In the home, the highest proportion of parents of students in the sample have finished secondary schools and have more than 200 books.

At school, students have enrolled in Economics because they regard it as useful for their future careers and it fits with the other subjects in which they are enrolled. The number of male and female students who elect to study Economics is the same as are their preferences regarding instructional techniques where both genders favour group discussions and small group work. The importance which students attribute to their schooling does not translate into their liking of either school in general or Economics in particular.

In general, student performance in Economics at both year levels is above average. Comparisons of achievement across a number of subgroups reveal that boys perform at higher levels than girls, who, in turn, show greater homogeneity in their performance than boys. At both year levels, students in urban areas (Year 11: N=540; Year 12: N=592) achieve significantly better in Economics than students in rural areas (Year 11: N=509; Year 12: N=555). The differences are noteworthy also for each of the subdomains. Likewise, noticeable differences are found between the school types with Independent school achieving at a higher level than Catholic or State schools.

Correlational analyses suggest that higher performing students have more positive attitudes to school in general and Economics in particular, higher educational expectations, spend less time pursuing jobs and watching TV and are from homes with higher socio-economic status.

Up to this point, the intended, implemented and attained curriculum were discussed separately. However, of particular interest to educational researchers and practitioners alike is the way in which the different components operate to influence Economics achievement. Only such an examination can lead to suggestions of changes aimed at improving learning outcomes in terms of student performance levels. To this end, results of analyses of complex models of student, teacher and school-level factors and their impact on each other and on student achievement are presented in the following chapter.

Chapter 5

Factors influencing economic literacy

This chapter combines information about the implemented and attained curriculum by means of analyses of models of student, teacher and school factors influencing achievement in Economics. Results presented in previous chapters reflected information on each of these factors separately or examined direct correlations between the factors and achievement.

The actual context in which student learning occurs, however, is more complex. Instructional techniques employed by teachers are dependent on resources provided by the school. Different instructional techniques lead to differences in students' appreciation of a particular subject. Time spent on homework by students is dependent on the amount and frequency of homework assigned by teachers. Socio-economic status of the home influences the amount of time students spend on different out-of-school activities such as sport or paid jobs.

Some of these relationships are direct while others operate indirectly. Thus, socio-economic status of the home may influence directly the amount of time students spend on different out-of-school activities, including homework. Time spent on homework, in turn, may affect level of achievement. As a consequence, achievement may be indirectly influenced by socio-economic status through the amount of time spent on homework. These are but a few examples of the complex relationships represented by models of educational achievement in which factors directly or indirectly influence each other and, ultimately, student learning.

In this chapter, models of factors influencing economic literacy which are developed based on prior research, logic and chronology will be analyzed. The analyses of the models will be conducted first at the student level, then at the school level. Finally, results will be presented of a simultaneous analysis of student and school-level information in one model.

Figure 5.1:   *Hypothesized   student-level   model*

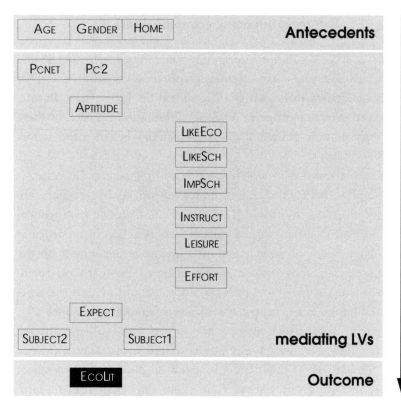

The idea to develop and analyze models of school achievement that take student, teacher and school factors into consideration was first introduced by Carroll (1963) and later extended by Bloom (1976), Harnischfeger and Wiley (1976), Reynolds and Walberg (1991) and Keeves (1992[2]). Extensive analyses of such models using data from large scale educational surveys have been reported by Keeves

(1992[1]), Kotte (1992), Lietz (1996), Lundberg and Linnakylä (1993) as well as Postlethwaite and Wiley (1991).

Based on results from the analyses of these models as well as findings of prior research into economic literacy (see Chapter 1) and correlational analyses presented in the previous chapter, a model of student-level factors influencing economics literacy has been developed. Figure 5.1 illustrates the proposed model of student-level factors influencing achievement in Economics.

Achievement in Economics, ECOLIT, as the outcome or criterion variable is located at the bottom of Figure 5.1. It is the construct of primary interest as the proposed model is designed to explain how student-level factors operate to explain differences in Economics achievement between students.

The top of Figure 5.1 illustrates that the model contains three antecedents namely HOME, GENDER and AGE. Antecedents are variables which are not considered to be influenced by any other factors in the model. Antecedents, like any other variables in the model are able to influence all subsequent variables in the model either directly or indirectly, through other, mediating, variables.

APTITUDE is perceived in the light of a definition given by Reynolds and Walberg (1991, p. 97). In their article on a structural model of science achievement they stated that...

"...the student aptitude-attributes set includes (a) student ability or prior achievement, (b) motivation, and (c) developmental level (e.g. age). This dimension is usually termed aptitude, referring to the attributes of students that are related to their academic performance. In this sense aptitude includes ability, motivation, and developmental level. In a technical sense, however, aptitude is restricted to cognitive ability".

Thus, APTITUDE is positioned straight after the antecedents but before any of the other mediating student-level variables. All other constructs with the exception of the outcome variable are considered to be mediating LVs. The attitudinal factors IMPSCH, LIKESCH and LIKEECO are assumed to precede the constructs INSTRUCT, LEISURE, EFFORT and EXPECT. In other words, it is hypothesized that the attitudes students have towards school in general and Economics in particular influence the amount of time students spend on leisure activities and homework. This commitment that upper secondary school students are prepared to make in turn, influences the choice of subjects in which students enrol (SUBJECT1, SUBJECT2). Finally, certain subjects (eg. Science, History) are considered to assist students' understanding of Economics more than others (e.g. Home Economics, Health Science). In summary, all constructs in the model can influence ECOLIT either directly or indirectly, through other, mediating, constructs.

The next step in the development of the model relates to the way in which indicators are combined into constructs. The purpose of creating such constructs is twofold. First, the combining of a number of variables which are considered to represent a common underlying concept increases the reliability of measurement. Instead of relying on information provided in response to just one item or question, data on several variables are combined to ensure that the concept is measured appropriately. Second, the forming of constructs or latent variables from manifest or observed variables allows the reduction of data to a manageable amount. Table 5.1 lists which manifest variables on which information was collected in the Economic Literacy Survey in 1998 have been used to form which constructs.

Thus, for example, the manifest variables mother's and father's education are combined with the number of books in the home to form the latent variable HOME. Likewise, watching TV, doing sports, amount of time spent on doing jobs at home and for pay constitute the construct LEISURE. The assigning of manifest variables to latent variables represents the outer model while the specification of the way in which constructs are assumed to influence achievement as proposed in Figure 5.1 is the inner model.

Table 5.1: *Latent variables and the number and type of manifest variables employed at the student level*

Construct	MVs	Specifications, manifest variable(s)
AGE	1	describes the student's age • age
GENDER	1	describes the student's gender • sex of student
HOME	3	reflects the socio-economic status of the student • father's educational level • mother's educational level • number of books at home
PC2	1	describes if a student has got a PC to work on at home • IBM compatible at home
PCNET	4	describes how a student uses the PC at home • use PC for communications • use PC for networking • use PC for word processing • use PC for other purposes
APTITUDE	2	comprises the student's last year performance at school • last year's result in English • last year's result in Mathematics
IMPSCH	4	reflects the importance a student ascribes to school • Important to do well at school • Important to do well in English • Important to do well in Mathematics • I can reach a satisfactory standard in my school work
LIKESCH	4	expresses the degree to which a student likes school • I get satisfaction from the school work I do • I like going to school • learning is fun • I enjoy being at school

(to be continued)

Table 5.1 (ctd.): Latent variables and the number and type of manifest variables employed at the student level

Construct	MVs	Specifications, manifest variable(s)
LIKEECO	6	expresses the degree to which a student likes Economics
		• I like Economics
		• Economics is useful for my future career
		• Economics should be compulsory
		• Economics is an easy subject
		• Economics is important to everyone's life
		• I would like to continue to study Economics after school
INSTRUCT	3	reflects to which degree certain forms of instruction are preferred
		• learning through group discussion
		• learning through individual study
		• learning through lectures
LEISURE	4	describes the amount of time spent on leisure activities
		• hrs watching TV
		• hrs doing sports
		• hrs working in paid job
		• hrs doing jobs at home
EFFORT	3	describes the efforts of students to do well in Economics
		• time spent on all homework
		• time spent on Economics homework
		• where getting knowledge from: Economics lessons
EXPECT	4	reflects the student's expectations to continue studying at tertiary level
		• expected educational level
		• why study Economics: I like the subject
		• why study Economics: It is useful for my future career
		• why study Economics: I wish to study the same subject as my friends

(to be continued)

100

Table 5.1 (ctd.): *Latent variables and the number and type of manifest variables employed at the student level*

Construct	MVs	Specifications, manifest variable(s)
SUBJECT1	2	describes if a student is also enrolled in other subjects
		• enrolled in Health Sciences
		• enrolled in Home Economics
SUBJECT2	2	describes if a student is also enrolled in other subjects
		• enrolled in Modern History
		• enrolled in Sciences
ECOLIT	1	outcome measure, ie. the economic literacy score
		• AUSTEL Rasch score

It should be noted that, in Figure 5.1, all variables earlier (ie. further up) in the model have the potential to influence any variable later (ie. further down) in the model, either directly or indirectly.

As a consequence, analysis of this model will allow the estimation of the relative effects of variables on each other as well as on economic literacy. Moreover, any emerging effects can be said to hold while all other effects are being held constant. In other words, if a direct effect emerged, for example, from GENDER to ECOLIT it would represent evidence to support the fact that gender differences in Economics occur even after other factors, such as time spent on homework or playing sports have been taken into account.

5.1.2 Analysis - Student-level model

This section presents the results of the analysis of the student-level model of factors influencing economics achievement proposed in Figure 5.1 using partial least squares path analysis (PLSPATH, Sellin 1990[1]). As a higher number of cases enhances the stability of estimates, it was decided to combine the information obtained from

Year 11 and Year 12 students. Scaling procedures based on IRT (see Section 4.2.5) were applied to the data to allow the equating of the performance of Year 11 and Year 12 students. As a result, student total test scores were brought to a common scale for the outcome variable ECOLIT used in the analysis. In order to allow the gain which occurred between Year 11 and Year 12 to be incorporated into the model, a dummy variable was included into the model. Preliminary results, however, showed that this variable did not affect any of the other variables in the model and was thus dropped from the analyses.

The final student-level model as computed with PLSPATH is shown in Figure 5.2. Only effect sizes or path coefficients of $|\beta| \geq 0.10$ are shown as this value is regarded as the minimum size for an effect not to be considered trivial (Cheung et al 1990; Keeves 1992[1]; Sellin 1990[2]). In the discussion of the sizes of path coefficients, Cohen (1969) has provided useful guidelines whereby coefficients between |0.10| and |0.25| are considered weak or small, between |0.25| and |0.40| medium, and values greater than |0.40| large or strong.

In Figure 5.2, effects between constructs which emerged from the analysis as non-trivial are indicated by an arrow ($\rightarrow$) where the head of the arrow symbolizes the direction of the effect. For example, results showed that GENDER had a direct effect on ECOLIT. It should be emphasized that while the results may provide supportive evidence of the hypothesized order they cannot be used to provide proof of causal effects.

The direct effects that are illustrated in Figure 5.2 are also presented in Table 5.2. In addition, Table 5.2 provides information on the total effects on a particular construct. Total effects include all direct effects on a particular construct plus effects which are mediated through other variables in the model.

So, what do the results tell us? Most noticeable is that all hypothesized constructs do, indeed, play a role in the model. Of the 15 constructs assumed to predict ECOLIT seven constructs have a direct effect on achievement, namely HOME ($\beta=0.10$), GENDER ($\beta=0.13$), PCNET

Figure 5.2:   Student-level model of factors influencing Economic Literacy

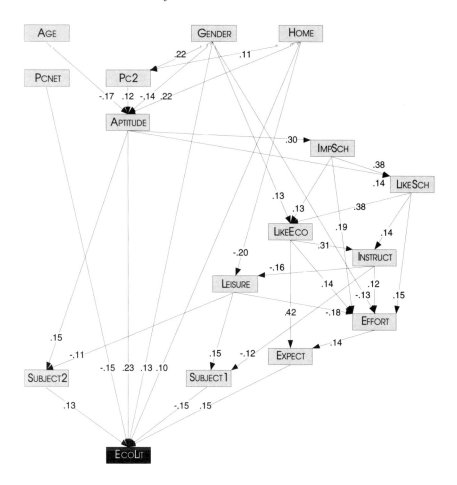

(β=0.15), APTITUDE (β=0.23), EXPECT (β=0.15), SUBJECT1 (β=0.15) and SUBJECT2 (β=0.13). Hence, the strongest predictor of economic literacy, is a student's aptitude as demonstrated in last year's performance in English and Mathematics.

Table 5.2: Direct and total effects of student-level factors

DIRECT EFFECTS ON	HOME	GENDER	AGE	PC2	PCNET	APTITUDE	IMPSCH	LIKESCH	LIKEECO	INSTRUCT	LEISURE	EFFORT	EXPECT	SUBJECT1	SUBJECT2
PC2	.11	.22	-	-	-	-	-	-	-	-	-	-	-	-	-
PCNET	-	-	-	-	-	-	-	-	-	-	-	-	-	-	-
APTITUDE	.22	-.14	-.17	.12	-	-	-	-	-	-	-	-	-	-	-
IMPSCH	-	-	-	-	-	.30	-	-	-	-	-	-	-	-	-
LIKESCH	-	-	-	-	-	.14	.38	-	-	-	-	-	-	-	-
LIKEECO	-	.13	-	-	-	-	.13	.38	-	-	-	-	-	-	-
INSTRUCT	-	-	-	-	-	-	-	.14	.31	-	-	-	-	-	-
LEISURE	-.20	-	-	-	-	-	-	-	-	-.16	-	-	-	-	-
EFFORT	-	-.13	-	-	-	-	-	.19	.15	.14	.12	-.18	-	-	-
EXPECT	-	-	-	-	-	-	-	-	.42	-	-	.14	-	-	-
SUBJECT1	-	-	-	-	-	-	-	-	-	-	-.12	.15	-	-	-
SUBJECT2	-	-	-	-	-	.15	-	-	-	-	-.11	-	-	-	-
ECOLIT	.10	.13	-	-	-.15	.23	-	-	-	-	-	-	.15	-.15	.13

TOTAL EFFECTS ON	HOME	GENDER	AGE	PC2	PCNET	APTITUDE	IMPSCH	LIKESCH	LIKEECO	INSTRUCT	LEISURE	EFFORT	EXPECT	SUBJECT1	SUBJECT2
PC2	.11	.22	-	-	-	-	-	-	-	-	-	-	-	-	-
PCNET	-	-	-	-	-	-	-	-	-	-	-	-	-	-	-
APTITUDE	.23	-.12	-.17	.12	-	-	-	-	-	-	-	-	-	-	-
IMPSCH	.07	-.03	-.05	.03	-	.30	-	-	-	-	-	-	-	-	-
LIKESCH	.06	-.03	-.04	.03	-	.25	.38	-	-	-	-	-	-	-	-
LIKEECO	.03	.12	-.02	.02	-	.13	.27	.38	-	-	-	-	-	-	-
INSTRUCT	.02	.03	-.01	.01	-	.08	.14	.26	.31	-	-	-	-	-	-
LEISURE	-.20	-.01	-	--	-	-.01	-.02	-.04	-.05	-.16	-	-	-	-	-
EFFORT	.06	-.12	-.02	.01	-	.12	.30	.24	.18	.14	-.18	-	-	-	-
EXPECT	.02	.03	-.01	.01	-	.07	.16	.19	.44	.02	-.02	.14	-	-	-
SUBJECT1	-.03	-.01	-	--	-	-.01	-.02	-.04	-.05	-.15	.15	-	-	-	-
SUBJECT2	.06	-.02	-.03	.02	-	.15	-	-	.01	.02	-.11	-	-	-	-
ECOLIT	.16	.11	-.04	.03	-.15	.26	.03	.03	.07	.03	-.04	.02	.15	-.15	.13

explained variance of ECOLIT (R^2):	24 %
overall explained variance of the model at student level:	9 %

This finding confirms previous results which have emphasized the importance of prior performance on current performance (Comber & Keeves 1973; Kotte 1992; Postlethwaite & Wiley 1991). The positive effect of high performance in English and Mathematics on Economics achievement is easily explained as higher performance in Economics and commonly requires the reading of study material and interpreting figures and tables.

 It is interesting to see that students' expectations about future involvement in Economics and tertiary studies as well as the specific subject choices appear to play a key role in differentiating between high and low achievers in Economics. Thus, a positive effect is recorded for EXPECT on ECOLIT which suggests that students who expect to proceed to tertiary level education perform at higher levels than those who do not share this expectation.

The subject choices students make at upper secondary level does make a difference. However, this choice does operate in opposite ways: students who have chosen to study Modern History and Science (SUBJECT2; positive path coefficient) seem to benefit with respect to their performance in Economics. In contrast, those students who are enrolled in Health Sciences and Home Economics (SUBJECT1; negative path coefficient) appear to perform at lower levels. In line with the argument in support of the positive effect of high performance in English and Mathematics, content covered in Modern History and Science is likely to be of greater assistance to the understanding of Economics than content taught in Health Sciences and Home Economics.

It should be noted for the interpretation of GENDER effects that because 'female' is coded as '1' and 'male' is coded as '2' a negative path coefficient indicates a superiority of female students whereas a positive effect represents a superiority of male students. A positive direct effect (β=0.13) emerges between gender and economic literacy which suggests that male students achieve at a higher level than female students even after other important factors, such as APTITUDE and HOME have been taken into account. Furthermore, girls put in greater effort (ie., GENDER→EFFORT, β=-0.13) while boys use more often, modern technology (GENDER→PC2, β=0.22).

Another noteworthy finding relates to the importance of attitudinal constructs, namely IMPSCH, LIKESCH, LIKEECO in the model. Thus, IMPSCH, LIKESCH, are influenced considerably by previous performance: The better students performed in the past the higher they rate the importance of school (APTITUDE→IMPSCH, β=0.30) and the more they like going to school (APTITUDE→LIKESCH, β=0.14).

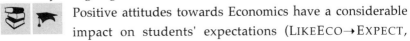 Positive attitudes towards Economics have a considerable impact on students' expectations (LIKEECO→EXPECT, β=0.42), which, in turn, contribute to higher performance in Economics. Likewise, positive attitudes lead to students favouring different types of Economics instruction (eg., LIKEECO→INSTRUCT, β=0.31).

Another noteworthy construct in the student-level model shown in Figure 5.2 is LEISURE. Though its total impact on ECOLIT is negligible it plays a vital role in 'linking' other LVs of the model. Both HOME (β=-0.20) and INSTRUCT (β=-0.16) have negative effects on LEISURE. In other words, students from lower socio-economic backgrounds tend to spend more time watching TV or doing jobs at home or for money which leaves less time for studies or homework in Economics.

It is, consequently, not surprising to find that LEISURE shows negative path coefficients both on EFFORT (β=-0.18) and on SUBJECT2 (β=-0.11) whereas the path on SUBJECT1 is positive (β=0.15). In other words, students who prefer to enjoy themselves in lots of leisure activities are more prone to invest less time on homework and are also more typically those students who stay away of academically more demanding subjects such as science or modern history.

As the results discussed here are based on an analysis of the combined sample of all upper secondary school students enrolled in Year 11 and Year 12 in Economics, AGE has been included in the model. This concept, however, does not play an important role in the student-level model.

Table 5.3:   *Factor loadings of manifest variables constituting*
              PCNET

MVs constituting PCNET	factor loading
PC is used for...	
communication packages	-.38
network management	.39
word-processing	-.51
other software	.56

The analyses provided some interesting results regarding the way in which PC usage impacts upon achievement. In order to facilitate interpretation of the construct PCNET, Table 5.3 provides details for the factor loadings of the four MVs which form PCNET.

While two of the activities load negatively on PCNET the other two MVs show a positive loading. This is important to know when interpreting the direct negative effect which PCNET has on ECOLIT (β=-0.15). Students who engage in using word-processing and communication software on their PCs achieve higher economic literacy scores than do students who use the PC mainly for non-specific purposes or network management.

When interpreting a path model it should be recognized that the overall explained variance of the model is only nine percent. In other words, 91 percent of the total variance of all LVs cannot be explained by this PLSPATH model. However, the amount of variance explained in the outcome variable, ECOLIT, suggests that the factors in the model account for 25 percent of the differences between high and low achievers in Economics. While not high, such amount of explained variance can be considered satisfactorily when compared with results of previous analyses of student-level models of educational achievement (eg. Lehmann et al 1995; Keeves 1992[1]; Lietz 1996).

107

5.2 School-level model of factors influencing economic literacy

5.2.1 Model development

In Chapter 3 information has been presented regarding the implemented Economics curriculum. In addition, the statistical analyses undertaken demonstrated which teacher- and school-related variables correlated with economic literacy. However, as stated previously, such bivariate correlations fail to take into account the more complex network of interrelationships between factors and the way in which they impact on each other to influence achievement. Hence, in this and the following section, a model of teacher and school-level factors influencing economic literacy is proposed and analyzed.

Figure 5.3:   Hypothesized school-level model

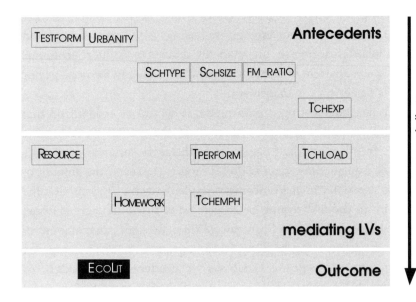

Table 5.4: *Latent variables and the number and type of manifest variables employed at the school level*

Construct	MVs	Specifications, manifest variable(s)
TESTFORM	1	specifies the type of Economic Literacy test taken • test form (paper & pencil, PC, WWW)
URBANITY	1	constitutes if a school is located in an urban or rural area • location of school (according to ABS classification)
SCHTYPE	1	describes the type of school • school type (State/Catholic/Independent school)
FM_RATIO	1	expresses the gender-ratio of the school at the upper secondary level • ratio of male to female students in Eco. at Year 11 and 12
SCHSIZE	6	describes the size of school • no. of male teachers • no. of female Econ. students enrolled at Year 11 in 1997 • no. of male Econ. students enrolled at Year 11 in 1997 • no. of female Econ. students enrolled at Year 12 in 1997 • no. of male Econ. students enrolled at Year 12 in 1997 • total enrolment at Year 11 in 1997
RESOURCE	1	describes the need for further resources as seen by the school principal • factor score of shortcomings reported
TCHEXP	1	defines the degree of experience of the Economics teacher • teaching experience in years
TCHLOAD	2	describes the teaching load of the Economics teacher • no. of Economics lessons at Year 11 • no. of Economics lessons at Year 12
TPERFORM	2	expresses the perceived level of performance the Economics teacher has of the students • expected performance of Year 11 students • expected performance of Year 12 students

(to be continued)

Table 5.4 (ctd.): *Latent variables and the number and type of manifest variables employed at the school level*

Construct	MVs	Specifications, manifest variable(s)
TCHEMPH	4	expresses emphasis put on teaching Economics • teacher uses charts for instruction • teacher puts emphasis on application processes • teacher puts emphasis on analytical processes • instruction comprises library work
HOMEWORK	3	summarizes to which degree homework is given in Economics • regularity of assigning homework in Economics • time it takes students at Year 11 to do homework in Eco. • time it takes students at Year 12 to do homework in Eco.
ECOLIT	1	outcome measure, ie. the economic literacy score • AUSTEL Rasch score (aggregated to school level)

Like the student-level model, the school-level model has been developed on the basis of prior research, logic and chronology. The reason for combining information collected from teachers and schools into one school-level model is that in only a few instances were questionnaires returned by more than one Economics teacher in a school. Figure 5.3 illustrates the hypothesized model of school-level factors influencing economic literacy.

Figure 5.3 shows that eleven constructs are proposed to influence achievement in Economics at the school-levels. Six antecedents, namely TESTFORM, URBANITY, SCHTYPE, SCHSIZE, FM_RATIO and TCHEXP are not assumed to be influenced by any other variables in the model. The mediating LVs include RESOURCE, TPERFORM, TCHLOAD, HOMEWORK and TCHEMPH. In other words, whether the school is located in an urban or rural area (URBANITY) is considered to have an impact on the type of resources available for teaching which, in turn, are assumed to influence performance in Economics. Likewise, the potential effect of teaching experience (TCHEXP) on achievement (ECOLIT) is hypothesized to be mediated by teaching emphasis. It should be noted that for the analysis of the school-level model students' performance in Economics has been aggregated so that one averaged score is used per school as the outcome measure (ECOLIT).

Table 5.4 provides an overview of how the theoretical constructs have been formed from manifest variables on which information was collected in the teacher and school background questionnaires in the Economic Literacy Survey in 1998.

Thus, for example, responses to questions regarding frequency and expected completion time of students' homework constitute the construct HOMEWORK at the school level. Furthermore, data regarding the use of different instructional techniques and emphasis on different process objectives are combined to form the construct TCHEMPH.

In this way, a model of school-level variables influencing Economics achievement was developed and subsequently analyzed using PLSPATH (Sellin 1990[1]).

5.2.2 Analysis - School-level model

Results of the direct effects which emerged between the proposed constructs for the final school-level model of factors influencing economic literacy is presented in Figure 5.4. In addition, Table 5.5 provides an overview of the direct and total effects of school-level factors.

 Seven of the eleven constructs in the model have a direct impact on the outcome measure. The strongest direct effect, though negative, is recorded for TCHLOAD ($\beta = -0.34$). This indicates that the higher the teaching load of an Economics teacher the less likely his or her class is to perform well. This makes sense in so far as a high teaching load may leave less room for comprehensive lesson preparation or a more varied didactical approach. Often teachers who are forced to teach many hours per week resort to textbooks or library tasks and repeat lessons using material from previous semesters rather than seeking to venture new instructional ideas by, for example, collecting up-to-date newspaper articles for group discussions or small-group work in Economics.

Figure 5.4: *School-level model of factors influencing Economic Literacy*

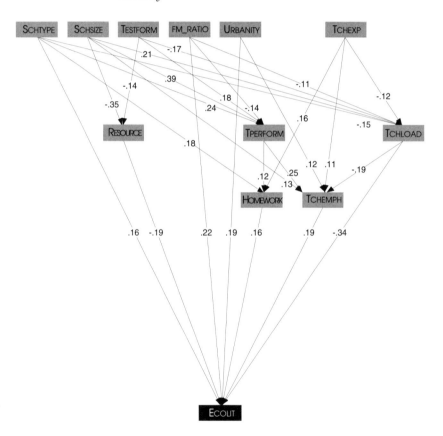

Table 5.5:   *Direct and total effects of school-level factors*

Direct Effects on	TESTFORM	URBANITY	SCHTYPE	TCHEXP	FM-RATIO	SCHSIZE	RESOURCE	TCHLOAD	TPERFORM	TCHEMPH	HOMEWORK
RESOURCE	-.14	-	-	-	-	-.35	-	-	-	-	-
TCHLOAD	-.17	-	-.15	-.11	-.11	.21	-	-	-	-	-
TPERFORM	.18	-	.24	-	-.14	.39	-	-	-	-	-
TCHEMPH	-	.12	-	.11	-	.13	-	-.19	.25	-	-
HOMEWORK	-	-	.18	.16	-	-	-	-	.12	-	-
ECOLIT	-	.19	.16	-	.22	-	-.19	-.34	-	.19	.16

Total Effects on	TESTFORM	URBANITY	SCHTYPE	TCHEXP	FM-RATIO	SCHSIZE	RESOURCE	TCHLOAD	TPERFORM	TCHEMPH	HOMEWORK
RESOURCE	-.14	-	-	-	-	-.35	-	-	-	-	-
TCHLOAD	-.17	-	-.15	-.11	-.11	.21	-	-	-	-	-
TPERFORM	.18	-	.24	-	-.14	.39	-	-	-	-	-
TCHEMPH	.08	.12	.09	.13	-.02	.18	-	-.19	.25	-	-
HOMEWORK	.02	-	.20	.16	-.02	.05	-	-	.12	-	-
ECOLIT	.10	.21	.26	.09	.25	.04	-.19	-.38	.07	.19	.16

explained variance of ECOLIT (R^2):	51 %
overall explained variance of the model at student level:	13 %

Positive direct effects on ECOLIT of similar strength emerge for FM_RATIO ($\beta=0.22$), URBANITY ($\beta=0.19$), TCHEMPH ($\beta=0.19$), SCHTYPE ($\beta=0.16$) and HOMEWORK ($\beta=0.16$). These findings indicate that the more male (Economics) students there are in a school/class (FM_RATIO) the more likely it is that the performance is high. This marks, most certainly, the high achievement of Independent boys-only schools and the fact that in coeducational classes the more able boys seem to select Economics in contrast to less able girls.

This is emphasized by the additional positive effect that SCHTYPE has on ECOLIT which suggests that Economics classes in Independent schools outperform those in Catholic and, to an even greater extent, in State schools. A cautionary note is in order here, in that descriptive statistics presented in Chapter 3 indicated that Independent schools were overrepresented in the sample which may partly explain these differences in achievement according to school type.

The location of the school (URBANITY) also appears to make a difference: rural schools are disadvantaged in comparison to the better achieving urban schools. It should be reiterated that this effect (like all other direct effects reported) emerges while all other effects in the model are kept constant. In this particular instance, it means that location does make a differences even after school type has been taken into account.

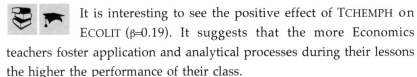 It is interesting to see the positive effect of TCHEMPH on ECOLIT ($\beta=0.19$). It suggests that the more Economics teachers foster application and analytical processes during their lessons the higher the performance of their class.

One other negative direct effect on ECOLIT measured at the school level emanates from RESOURCE ($\beta=0.19$). In schools where the school principal acknowledges the need for further resources such as instructional software or PCs, performance in Economics is lower than in schools for which no such shortcomings are reported.

Interesting information can also be derived from an examination of the direct effects between the predicting constructs. The size of school, for example, impacts strongly and negatively on the shortcomings noted by the school principal (SCHSIZE→RESOURCE; $\beta=0.35$) underscoring that the larger schools are more likely to encounter limitations with respect to teaching facilities and instructional materials.

Results also show that classes in larger schools are slightly disadvantaged because teachers in these schools have a noticeably higher teaching load (β=0.21) which, as pointed out above, impacts negatively on the Economics achievement of their classes. In contrast, classes taught in smaller schools are more likely to benefit from the lower teaching load of Economics teachers in these schools.

The school-level model identifies a direct path from TCHEXP on HOMEWORK (β=0.16) which, in turn, directly influences ECOLIT (β=0.16). This means that the more experienced Economics teachers tend to give more homework to their students which, in turn, fosters the achievement of their classes. At the same time, teaching load operates as a mediating variable whereby less experienced teachers have higher teaching loads (β=0.12) with such higher loads contributing to classes achieving below average (β=0.34).

Finally, as can be seen in Table 5.5, the explained variance (R^2) of economic literacy amounts to 51 percent. This is a satisfactory result even if the overall model accounts for only 13 of the total variance. This is not unexpected and in line with earlier path models designed for other subject areas at school-level (Keeves & Kotte 1995; Kotte 1992; Lietz 1996; Postlethwaite & Wiley 1991).

5.3   Hierarchical linear model

In the above analyses, data collected at the student level and at the school level were examined separately. This was done because the technique employed for analysis, namely PLSPATH (Sellin 1990[1]) is a single-level technique which means that data can be analyzed at only one level at a time. In order for data collected at different levels to be combined into a single-level analysis, information from the lower (ie. student) level would have to be aggregated to the higher (ie. school) level. Or, school-level data would have to be disaggregated to the student level. Estimates of effects, however, are likely to be biased where data obtained at different levels are examined with single level analytical techniques (Cheung et al 1990; Cheung & Tsoi 1990; Sellin 1990[2]). Hence, in this section a model is developed and analyzed which takes into account the nested structure of the data.

Hierarchical linear modelling (HLM) or multilevel modelling represents and attempt to take into consideration the nested structure of educational data which is inevitable as students are usually taught within classes, classes are nested within schools and schools are grouped fro administrative purposes, for example, according to regions (Raudenbush & Willms 1991).

Figure 5.5:   *Hierarchical linear model of factors influencing Economic Literacy*

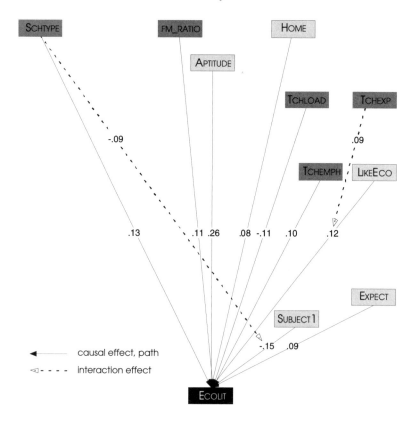

Table 5.6:   *Final estimation of fixed effects; two-level HLM model*

Fixed Effect on→ECOLIT	Coefficient (γ)	Standard Error	T-ratio	P-value
Level 2/school-level effects				
SCHTYPE	0.127	0.034	3.751	0.000
FM_RATIO	0.112	0.033	3.420	0.001
TCHLOAD	-0.112	0.038	-2.926	0.004
TCHEMPH	0.097	0.039	2.461	0.014
Level 1/student-level effects				
HOME	0.078	0.035	2.248	0.025
APTITUDE	0.262	0.033	7.840	0.000
EXPECT	0.090	0.032	2.786	0.006
LIKEEO	0.121	0.031	3.928	0.000
interaction effect by TCHEXP	0.095	0.034	2.770	0.006
SUBJECT1	-0.151	0.034	-4.457	0.000
interaction effect by SCHTYPE	-0.087	0.034	-2.569	0.011

Note:
   for further information see Bryk, Raudenbush & Congdon 1996

Different procedures that seek to take the multilevel nature of most educational data sets into account have been developed (Aitkin & Longford 1986; Goldstein 1987; Raudenbush & Bryk 1986). For reasons of relative ease of application and interpretation of results, the computer program HLM 4.01 which was developed by Bryk, Raudenbush and Congdon (1996) has been used in the analysis of the two-level hierarchical model of factors influencing economic literacy. Results of the analysis are presented in Figure 5.5 and Tables 5.6 and 5.7.

Table 5.7:   *Estimation of variance components - two-level HLM model*

Model	Estimation of variance components between	
	students ($\hat{\sigma}^2$)	schools ($\hat{\tau}_\pi$)
number of cases	1467	74
fully unconditional model	0.88	0.12
unconditional model at level-2	0.72	0.11
final two-level model	0.72	0.06

Variance at each level

between-students: $\dfrac{\hat{\sigma}^2 [\text{fully unc.}]}{(\hat{\tau}_{00}[\text{fully unc.}] + \hat{\sigma}^2[\text{fully unc.}])} = \dfrac{0.88}{(0.12 + 0.88)} = \dfrac{0.88}{1.00} = \mathbf{0.88}$

between-schools: $\dfrac{\hat{\tau}_{00}[\text{fully unc.}]}{(\hat{\tau}_{00}[\text{fully unc.}] + \hat{\sigma}^2[\text{fully unc.}])} = \dfrac{0.12}{(0.12 + 0.88)} = \dfrac{0.12}{1.00} = \mathbf{0.12}$

Proportion of variance explained by final model

between-students $\dfrac{(\hat{\sigma}^2[\text{fully unc.}] - \hat{\sigma}^2[\text{final}])}{\hat{\sigma}^2[\text{fully unc.}]} = \dfrac{(0.88 - 0.72)}{0.88} = \dfrac{0.16}{0.88} = \mathbf{0.18}$

between-schools $\dfrac{(\hat{\tau}_\pi[\text{fully unc.}] - \hat{\tau}_\pi[\text{final}])}{\hat{\tau}_\pi[\text{fully unc.}]} = \dfrac{(0.12 - 0.06)}{0.12} = \dfrac{0.06}{0.12} = \mathbf{0.50}$

Table 5.6 shows that five level-1 variables influence Economics achievement, namely students' home background (HOME; $\gamma=0.08$), prior achievement (APTITUDE; $\gamma=0.26$), liking of Economics (LIKEECO; $\gamma=0.12$), expectations regarding further education (EXPECT; $\gamma=0.09$), and enrolment in Home Economics or Health Science (SUBJECT1; $\gamma=-0.15$). This evidence largely confirms the results of the student-level PLSPATH analyses (see Section 5.1.2) which revealed direct positive effects on achievement from HOME, APTITUDE and EXPECT and a negative effect from SUBJECT1 with APTITUDE as the strongest predictor of economic literacy. It should be noted that the significance tests in HLM take into account the different numbers of cases at the student and school level. Thus, effect sizes reported here are not subject to any aggregation bias and, hence, student and school effects can be directly compared.

 At the school level, four significant effects are reported. Thus, school type (SCHTYPE γ=0.13), the gender ratio of the school (FM_RATIO; γ=0.11), teaching load (TCHLOAD; γ=-0.11) and teaching emphasis (TCHEMPH; γ=0.10) are demonstrated to have an impact on achievement. Again, these effects largely confirm the results of the PLSPATH analyses in that students in schools which are independent, have larger proportions of male students, with teachers who have lower teaching loads and focus on application and analysis perform at higher levels than other students.

Finally, two interaction effects in this two-level hierarchical model should be noted, namely one of TCHEXP on LIKEECO (γ=0.09) and one of SCHTYPE on SUBJECT1 (γ=-0.09). The first and positive effect indicates that students' liking of Economics has an even greater differentiating effect between high and low achievers in classes that are taught by more experienced teachers. The second and negative effect suggests that enrolment in Home Economics or Health Science differentiates even more between high and low achievers in Economics in State schools.

Table 5.7 illustrates that 88 percent of the variance in economic literacy is associated with the student level while 12 percent can be attributed to the school level. This proportion of student-level variance is slightly higher than in previous analyses of Australian data (OECD 1998, p. 327) which showed about three quarters of the total variance to be associated with the student level.

The final two-level hierarchical model accounts for 18 percent of the variance between students while half the variance at the school level is explained. These proportions of explained variance are comparable with results of analyses of previous two-level modelling using HLM (Lietz 1996).

5.4 Summary

Path analyses as well as hierarchical linear modelling are statistical approaches which are meant to summarize information in a meaningful way identifying, where possible, causal effects between the constructs. The analyses presented in this chapter illustrated that there is a set of factors operating to influence economic literacy among students at the upper secondary school level. The way these factors increase or decrease student performance in Economics appears to be a complex network of causal relationships and interdependencies of student, teacher and school effects. Only by introducing state-of-the-art multilevel modelling is it possible to simultaneously estimate the different effect sizes of each of the constructs.

  Path analyses at the student level showed, not surprisingly, that the student's general scholastic aptitude proved to be the strongest predictor in fostering economic literacy. However, it should be noted that positive attitudes towards Economics and high expectations to resume further tertiary studies also play a key role in stimulating economic literacy. This finding should alert educators to think of and implement strategies how to enhance students' interest and motivation to study Economics, perhaps by demonstrating to them - and their parents - the importance of being knowledgable about economic matters. Building positive attitudes towards Economics is a first, but very important step, it seems to increase students' levels of economic literacy.

Since Economics is still an elective subject at the upper secondary school level it is not coincidental that the path analyses discussed above underscored that the subject choice a student makes does indeed have an effect on his or her level of performance in Economics. It can be argued that content covered in Modern History and Science is likely to be of greater assistance to the understanding of economic matters. Conversely, opting for Health Sciences and Home Economics does seem to have a negative impact on the level of economic literacy.

But apart from these student-level effects it was interesting to the extent to which high teaching load can negatively affect the class performance in Economics. Economics teachers burdened with a heavy teaching load are prone not to teach as effectively as those with less hours of teaching obligations. The results also showed that students of teachers who foster application and analytical processes in their instruction are likely to achieve higher levels of economic literacy.

 The HLM analyses presented here confirmed clearly the preliminary findings obtained by the path analyses run separately for the student and school level. As regards economic literacy, Independent schools demonstrate considerably higher performance than State and Catholic schools. At the same time, in predominantly male classrooms achievement in Economics appears to be higher. However, a larger sample may be needed to verify this gender bias.

The path models proposed, analyzed and discussed for the student and school level as well as the simultaneous, two-level HLM model designed in Figure 5.5 are by no means a perfect reflection of reality since they can only explain a relatively modest amount of variance of students, teacher and school variables. Nevertheless, the results should be taken as a useful starting point to develop personal, curricular and administrative strategies and policies which may benefit the level of performance in economic literacy. A relatively easy starting point may be (a) the promotion of positive attitudes among students and parents by emphasizing the importance of economic literacy and (b) the reduction of teaching loads of Economics teachers.

Chapter 6

The future of economic literacy

In this final chapter, implications of the information presented in this book for the future of economic literacy are discussed. It considers the major points which have emerged from the detailed analysis of the intended, implemented and attained Economics curriculum at the upper secondary school level. As a consequence, it provides food for thought and action for school principals, teachers, policy and decision-makers as well as educational researchers who are interested in furthering Economics education at the senior secondary school level in order for students to become informed adults who are able to evaluate economic policies and decision making.

The importance of developing students to become economically literate adults is reflected in the fact that all Australian States and Territories provide students with the opportunity to study Economics at the upper secondary school levels. Statements of curricular intent reflect clearly the significance of the need for basic skills and abilities in the area of economic thinking to make informed decisions about personal issues regarding study, work and personal investment as well as societal issues such as the evaluation of political choices and business opportunities.

6.1 Intended is not always attained

While the Economics curricula are not identical across Australia, a content analysis of the different curricular documents reveals a large common core of economic concepts. Thus, Fundamental Economics which covers concepts such as scarcity, opportunity costs, productivity and economic systems is usually covered in Year 11. Likewise,

Microeconomics which includes concepts such as markets and prices, supply and demand, income distribution and market failures is covered as a core area in Year 11. The Year 12 curricula deal with macroeconomic concepts, for example, gross national product, aggregate supply and demand as well as fiscal and monetary policy. In addition, International Economic Concepts in terms of comparative advantage, barriers to trade, balance of payment and international growth are covered in Year 12. This is not to suggest, however, that the economic concepts covered in Year 11 will not be taken up again in Year 12. The curricular analysis provides evidence of a somewhat spiral approach whereby previously covered concepts may be reintroduced at a later stage but rather than mere repetition, the focus is on developing further an appreciation of the complexity and interrelatedness of different economic concepts.

In addition to the common core, the content analysis also revealed a number of elective topics which cover issues that are of particular interest in the economy of a State, for example, forestry, agriculture or mining.

A test instrument to assess the extent to which the intended curriculum has been attained was developed using the *Test of Economic Literacy* (Soper & Walstad, 1987) as a basis. The TEL was developed in the US and normed in a nationwide assessment. Great care and extensive piloting showed that the TEL could be readily adapted to the Australian context. The fact that only minor changes had to be made enabled some, though limited, comparisons with performance levels measured by the TEL in other countries.

Results of the Economic Literacy Survey - Queensland 1998 suggested that, overall, Economics students achieved at a satisfactory level. While the study was not designed to enable direct comparisons, it can be concluded that Queensland's students achieved at the same level as their counterparts in the United States.

Economics students in Queensland performed above average especially in the areas of Macroeconomics in Year 11 and Microeconomics in Year 12 which runs somewhat counter to the intended curriculum coverage of these two concept areas at the two year levels. The fact that a number of microeconomic concepts are reintroduced and discussed in greater detail in Year 12 may account for these results. At both year levels, the greatest differences between high and low performers were recorded in the content area of Macroeconomics. Achievement levels in International Economics are somewhat lower which suggests room for improvement, particularly if Australia seeks to prepare its citizens well for global competition in international markets.

Economics in Australia is not yet perceived as a key competency such as English or Mathematics and remains an elective subject only available at the upper secondary school level. It should be borne in mind that the performance levels reported in this study are based on students who were enrolled in Economics. Hence, results reported in this book do not provide any account of the levels of economic literacy of the majority of students who have decided to enrol in other subjects.

This survey also shed light on the performance differences between certain subgroups. A look at the three school types illustrates the not unexpected finding that students in Independent school score significantly better than students enrolled in State schools. These results hold also when other important factors such as student aptitude, home background, teaching experience and teaching loads are taken into consideration.

Evidence emerged indicating that male students outperformed female students. This finding applied when comparing achievement scores between boys and girls as well as when analyzing the student model of factors influencing economic literacy which, among other things, took into account leisure time activities and homework effort. In contrast, no gender differences emerged with respect to attitudes regarding economic issues in general and the school subject of

Economics in particular. Likewise, all Economics students, regardless of gender, assigned great importance to school in general and English and Mathematics in particular. In contrast, Economics was considered to be less important. This finding is of particular concern given that this view was expressed by students who were enrolled in Economics. It suggests that their study of the topic does not result in an increased appreciation of the relevance of economic matters.

It is encouraging to find that most Economics teachers perceive themselves to be adequately trained. Comparisons with US findings show that on average, Queensland Economics teachers have higher levels of subject specific education than Economics teachers in the US. The confidence derived from this education is reflected by the majority of Queensland teachers feeling quite capable to use current newspaper articles as the basis for instruction. The Economics teacher cohort reports similar proportions of male and female teachers who know what to expect of their students. Most teachers can predict the performance level of their students relatively accurately. However, common forms of instruction in Economics are still lecturing, library work and group discussions. Modern media, such as the internet, are rarely used which suggests that there is room for improvement in terms of the way in which the Economics curriculum is implemented.

6.2 Room for improvement

The path analyses conducted separately at the student and school level identified several factors contributing to differences in performance levels in Economics. In order to appropriately take into account the different levels at which information was collected and the different numbers of students and schools that participated in the Economic Literacy Survey, a two-level hierarchical linear analysis was undertaken. This analysis allowed the simultaneous estimation of the relative effects of student and school-level factors on economic literacy.

126

The multilevel analyses supported the results of separate single-level analyses of student and school models of factors influencing achievement in Economics.

 Results of the analysis revealed that students who had performed previously at higher levels in English and Mathematics were also more likely to demonstrate above average scores in Economics. In addition, students with higher expectations regarding future education and more favourable attitudes towards Economics tended to perform significantly better. Not surprisingly the socio-economic background of the students contributed positively to a higher economic literacy score. Finally, results indicated that enrolment in Health Sciences or Home Economics did not improve Economics performance whereas students enrolled in Modern History and Science demonstrated higher levels of economic literacy.

Important teacher factors influencing student performance included teaching load and teaching emphasis. Thus, students who were taught by teachers with lighter teaching loads who put greater emphasis on processes of application and analysis performed at higher levels.

With regard to school-level variables the study found that students in larger schools and in Independent schools obtained higher scores. In other words, students in smaller schools as well as in State and Catholic schools are somewhat disadvantaged and consideration may be given to policies aimed at addressing these differences.

For reasons of brevity and stimulation of discussion the main findings of the study are provided in terms of an executive summary on the following page.

6.3 Executive summary

 The 12 major findings of the *Economic Literacy Survey - Queensland 1998* are that...

- students who do well in English and Mathematics are also likely to perform well in Economics
- male students perform better than female students
- students with a higher socio-economic background achieve at a higher level in Economics
- positive attitudes towards Economics and school in general as well as higher tertiary study expectations lead to increased performance
- Queensland's Year 11 and Year 12 Economics students are doing at least as well in Economics as their counterparts in United States high schools
- the increase in achievement levels from Year 11 to Year 12 is in line with expectations and is similar to gains in other subject areas
- teaching under a high teaching load is detrimental to students' performance in Economics
- the teacher's gender does not make any difference to the performance of male or female students in Economics
- students taught by teachers who assign greater emphasis on cognitive learning processes such as application and analysis achieve at a higher level in Economics
- Independent schools perform significantly better than State schools
- assessment of economic literacy by paper & pencil, stand-alone PC or the internet produces results of comparable reliability and validity.

6.4 The outlook

This book represents a systematic analysis of Economics education at the upper secondary school level through an examination of the intended, implemented and attained curriculum. Details of the intended curriculum are derived from a content analysis of the Economics curricula of all Australian States and Territories. Information regarding the implemented and attained curriculum is obtained from 74 schools and 1,467 students in Queensland. Information was synthesized through the analysis of models of student, teacher and school factors influencing achievement. Analyses included the application of a multilevel analytical technique (HLM) which took into account the nested structure of the collected data and the different numbers of cases at the student and school levels.

 In this context, it is noteworthy that the study of the attained curriculum was the first in Australia to successfully measure levels of economic literacy on a valid and reliable test that provided students, teachers and school with the flexibility to participate using paper and pencil, stand alone PCs or the internet. Geographically and logistically, the study covered an area that was many times larger than most European countries. Yet, the turnaround time between data collection and reporting of results was minimal as information was obtained from students, teachers and school principals via PC and the internet. This effectiveness suggests that the use of the internet for data collection is a significant step forward in the conduct of large-scale school surveys.

It is considered essential to obtain accurate information regarding the performance of upper secondary students in all States and Territories to examine whether or not the findings from the Queensland-wide survey apply across Australia. Moreover, it would be of immense interest to compare the intended, implemented and attained Economics curricula in an international study of economic literacy. Evidence of the analyses of the different Economics curricula in Australia - where each State and Territory has the authority to design and implement its own curriculum - suggests a sufficiently large common core to warrant an international survey.

Finally, this survey has demonstrated the importance of knowledge in Economics for the interpretation and evaluation of everyday events. Hence, it would be highly desirable to include a basic knowledge about economic matters into the compulsory part of the curriculum. At present, only some students have the opportunity to develop economic literacy as Economics is an elective subject. As a consequence, the majority of Australian school leavers remain uninformed and not well equipped when it comes to evaluating the economic implications of different political and electoral options concerning society as well as their personal lives in terms of further study, work, and money matters.

The basic economic concept is the problem of choice whereby societies have to decide how to use their limited resources to satisfy their continuing needs. Likewise, as Nobel Laureate James Tobin has emphasized, individuals have to make economic decisions all their lives. Developments in information technology mean that these choices are not restricted to or influenced by the immediate environment. Instead, they are taken in an international and global context where individuals are confronted with and have access to information from around the world. This book has shown that the contemporary Economics education in Australia is a good starting point to provide school leavers with the necessary knowledge and skills for a critical evaluation of these very choices.

References

Adams, R.J. & Khoo, S.K. 1993, Quest - The interactive test analysis system, Australian Council for Educational Research, Hawthorn, Vic.

Aitkin, M. & Longford, N. 1986, 'Statistical modeling issues in school effectiveness studies (with discussion)', Journal of the Royal Statistical Society, Series A, vol. 149, pp. 1-42.

Anderson, B. et al. 1986, Homework: What do national assessment results tell us? National Assessment of Educational Progress, Princeton, NJ. Center for Statistics (OERI/ED), Washington, DC. NAEP-15-R-03. Abstract from ERIC database, item ED276980.

Beck, K. 1993 Dimensionen der ökonomischen Grundbildung. Meßinstrumente und Befunde [Abschlußbericht zum DFG-Projekt (Az. II A 4 – Be 1077/3: Wirtschaftskundlicher Bildungs-Test. Normierung und internationaler Vergleich). Universität Erlangen-Nürnberg, Wirtschafts- und sozialwissenschaftliche Fakultät, Betriebswirtschaftliches Institut, Nürnberg.

Beck, K. & Krumm, V. 1991, 'Economic literacy in German speaking countries and the United States. First steps to a comparative study', Economia, vol. 1, no. 1, pp. 17-23.

Beck, K. & Krumm, V. 1990, Economic Literacy in the United States, Germany, and Austria: Results of Cross National Studies. Paper presented at the Annual Meeting of the Joint Council on Economic Education/National Association of Economic Educators (Los Angeles, CA, September). ERIC doc. ref. ED340629.

Beck, K. & Krumm, V. 1989, Economic literacy in German speaking countries and the United States. First steps to a comparative study. Paper presented at the annual meeting of American Education Research Association, San Francisco.

Becker, W. 1997, 'Teaching economics to undergraduates', Journal of Economic Literature, vol. 35, pp. 1347-1373.

Becker, W., Greene, W. & Rosen, S. 1990, 'Research on high school economic education', Journal of Economic Education, vol. 21, no. 3.

Bell, E. & Williams, J. 1997, Student participation and Student Outcomes in the Social Sciences, Queensland Board of Senior Secondary School Studies, Brisbane.

Berelson, B. 1952, Content analysis in communication research, Free Press, Glencoe, Il.

Bloom, B.S. 1976, Human characteristics and school learning, McGraw-Hill, New York.

Board of Senior Secondary School Studies Australian Capital Territory, 1995, Economics course framework, Australian Capital Territory, Department of Education and Training, Canberra.

Board of Senior Secondary School Studies Queensland 1992, Senior syllabus in economics, Board of Senior Secondary School Studies Queensland, Spring Hill.

Board of Studies, New South Wales, 1994, Stage 6 syllabus Economics 2/3 Unit preliminary and HSC courses, Board of Studies, Sydney, New South Wales.

Board of Studies, Victoria, 1994, Economics, VCE Study design, Board of Studies, Carlton, Victoria.

Bodenhausen, J. 1988, Does the academic background of teachers affect the performance of their students?, Abstract from ERIC database, item ED293836.

Bryk, A., Raudenbush, S. & Congdon, R. 1996, HLM: Hierarchical linear and nonlinear modeling with the HLM/2L and HLM/3L programs, SSI Scientific Software International, Chicago, Il.

Buckles, M. & Watts, S. 1998, 'National standards in economics, history, social studies, civics, and geography: Complementarities, competition, or peaceful coexistence?' Journal of Economic Education, vol. 29, no. 2, pp. 157-162.

Carroll, J.B. 1975, The teaching of French as a foreign language in eight countries, Almqvist and Wiksell, Stockholm, Sweden and Wiley, New York.

Caroll, J.B. 1963, 'A model of school learning', Teachers College Record, 64, pp. 723-733.

Cheung, K. C. & Tsoi, S.C. 1990, 'Model specification and related issues' in K.C. Cheung et al. 1990 op. cit. pp. 233-244.

Cheung, K.C., Keeves, J.P., Sellin, N. & Tsoi, S.C. 1990, 'The analysis of multilevel data in educational research: Studies of problems and their solutions', International Journal of Educational Research, vol. 14, no. 3, Pergamon Press, Oxford.

Cohen, J. 1969, Statistical power analysis for the behavioural sciences. Academic Press, New York.

Comber, L.C. & Keeves, J.P. 1973, Science education in nineteen countries. International studies in evaluation I, Almqvist and Wiksell, Stockholm.

Curriculum Council of Western Australia 1998, Economics (Year 11) - D304 [online]. Available at URL: http://www.curriculum.wa.edu.au/pages/subj/subj304.htm.

Curriculum Council of Western Australia 1998, Economics (Year 12) - E304 [online]. Available at URL: http://www.curriculum.wa.edu.au/pages/subj/subj304.htm.

Department of Education, Queensland 1991, Managing curriculum development in Queensland. Report submitted to the Minister for Education. Publishing Service: Department of Education, Queensland, Brisbane.

Elley, W.B. (ed.) 1994, The IEA study of reading literacy: Achievement and instruction in thirty-two school systems, Pergamon Press, Oxford.

Elley, W.B. 1992, How in the world do students read? The International Association for the Evaluation of Educational Achievement, The Hague, The Netherlands.

Ellison, A. & Kallenback, S. 1996, 'Political and economic literacy', Adult Learning, May/June 1996, pp. 26-27.

Gleason, J. & van Scyoc, L.J. 1995, 'A report on the economic literacy of adults', Research in Economic Education, Summer, pp. 203-210.

Goldstein, H. 1987, Multilevel models in educational and social research, Oxford University Press, New York.

Grimes, P.W. & Register, C.A. 1990, 'Teachers' unions and student achievement in high school economics', Journal of Economic Education, vol. 21, no. 3.

Hallows, K. & Becker, W.E. 1994, 'What works and what doesn't: A practitioner's guide to research findings in economic education.' International Journal of Social Education, vol. 8, no. 3, pp. 87-95.

Hansen, W.L. 1998, 'Principles-based standard: On the voluntary national content standard in economics', Journal of Economic Education, vol. 29, no. 2, pp. 150-154.

Hansen, W.L. et al. 1977, A framework for teaching economics: Basic concepts, Joint Council on Economic Education, New York.

Harnischfeger, A. & Wiley, D.E. 1976, 'The teaching-learning process in elementary schools: A synoptic view', Curriculum Inquiry, vol. 6, pp. 5-43.

Highsmith, R.J. 1990, 'How do we stand in high school economics today?' Social Education, vol. 54, no. 2, pp. 81-83.

Holsti, O.R. 1969, Content analysis for the social sciences and humanities, Addison-Wesley, Reading, Mass.

Huskey, L., Jackstadt, S.L. & Goldsmith, S. 1991, 'Economic literacy and the content of television network news', Social Education, March, pp. 182 - 185.

Keeves, J.P. 1996, The world of school learning. Selected key findings from 35 years of IEA research, The International Association for the Evaluation in Educational Achievement, The Hague, The Netherlands.

Keeves, J.P. 1992[1], Learning Science in a Changing World. Cross-national studies of Science Achievement: 1970 to 1984. The International Association for the Evaluation in Educational Achievement, The Hague, The Netherlands.

Keeves, J.P. 1992[2], The IEA study of science III: Changes in science education and achievement: 1970 to 1984, Pergamon, Oxford.

Keeves, J.P. & Kotte, D. 1995, 'Patterns of science achievement: International comparisons' in Gender, science and mathematics. Shortening the shadow, ed. L.H. Parker, L.J. Rennie & B.J. Fraser, Kluwer, Hingham, MA.

Kotte, D. 1992, Gender differences in science achievement in 10 countries - 1970/71 to 1983/84, Peter Lang, Frankfurt.

Kotte, D. & Lietz, P. 1998, 'Welche Faktoren beeinflussen die Leistung in Wirtschaftskunde?' Zeitschrift für Berufs- und Wirtschaftspädagogik, vol. 94, no. 10, pp. 421-434.

Krippendorf, K. 1980, Content analysis. An introduction to its methodology, Sage Publications, Beverly Hills.

Lambin, R. 1995, 'What can planners expect from international quantitative studies?' in Reflections on educational achievement. Papers in honour of T. Neville Postlethwaite, eds. W. Bos & R.H. Lehmann, Waxmann, Münster/New York.

Lehmann, R.H., Peek, R., Pieper, I., & von Stritzky, R. 1995, Leseverständnis und Lesegewohnheiten deutscher Schülerinnen und Schüler, Beltz Verlag, Weinheim/Basel, Switzerland.

Lietz, P. 1996, Reading comprehension across cultures and over time, Waxmann, Münster/New York.

Lietz, P. & Kotte, D. 1997, Economic literacy in Central Queensland: Results of a pilot study, paper presented at the Australian Association for Research in Education (AARE) annual meeting, December, Brisbane.

Lietz, P. & Kotte, D. 1999, 'Gender differences in economics: Fact or artefact?' Journal of Research and Development in Education. vol. 32, no. 4., pp. 213-223.

Lokan, J., Ford, P. & Greenwood, L. 1996, Maths & science on the line: Australian junior secondary students' performance in the Third International Mathematics and Science Study, Australian Council for Educational Research, Melbourne.

Lokan J, Ford, P. & Greenwood, L. 1997, Maths & science on the line: Australian middle primary students' performance in the Third International Mathematics and Science Study, Australian Council for Educational Research, Melbourne.

Lundberg, I. & Lynnakylä, P. 1993, Teaching reading around the world, International Association for the Evaluation of Educational Achievement, Hamburg, Germany.

Madaus, G.F., Airasian, P.W. & Kellaghan, T. 1980, School effectiveness. A reassessment of the evidence, McGraw-Hill, New York.

Marsh, C.J. 1994, Producing a national curriculum. Plans and paranoia, Allen & Unwin, St Leonards.

Martin, M.O. & Kelly, D.A. (eds) 1996, Third international mathematics and science study technical report, volume II design and development. Primary and middle school years. Center for the Study of Testing, Evaluation, and Educational Policy, Boston College, Chestnut Hill, MA, & International Association for the Evaluation of Educational Achievement (IEA), Amsterdam.

Tobin, J. 1986 'Economic Literacy Isn't Marginal Investment', Wall Street Journal, edition 9 July 1986.

Organisation for Economic Cooperation and Development (OECD) 1998, Education at a glance. OECD indicators. OECD, Paris.

Paschal, R.A., Weinstein, T., & Walberg, H.J. 1984, 'The effects of homework on learning: A quantitative synthesis', Journal of Educational Research, vol. 78, no. 2, pp. 97-104.

Postlethwaite, T.N. & Ross, K.N. 1992, Effective schools in reading. Implications for educational planners, International Association for the Evaluation of Educational Achievement, Hamburg, Germany.

Postlethwaite, T.N. & Wiley, D.E. 1991, Science Achievement in Twenty-Three Countries, Pergamon Press, Oxford.

Rader, W.D. 1996, 'Toward a philosphy of economics education', The Social Studies, vol. 87, pp. 4-6.

Rasch, G. 1960, Probabilistic models for some intelligence and attainment tests, Danmarks Paedagogiske Institute, Copenhagen, Denmark.

Raudenbush, S.W. & Bryk, A.S. 1986, 'A hierarchical model for studying school effects', Sociology of Education, vol. 59, no. 1, pp. 1-17.

Raudenbush, S.W. & Willms, J.D. 1991, 'The organisation of schooling and its methodological implications' in Schools, classrooms and pupils. International studies of schooling from a multilevel perspective, eds. S.W. Raudenbush & J.D. Willms, Academic Press, San Diego.

Reynolds, A. J. & Walberg, H. J. 1991, 'A structural model of science achievement', Journal of Educational Psychology, vol. 83, no. 1, pp. 97-107.

Robitaille, D.F. & Garden, R.A. 1989, The IEA study of mathematics II: Contexts and outcomes of school mathematics, Pergamon, Oxford.

Rosier, M.J. & Keeves, J.P. (ed.) 1991, The IEA study of science I: Science education and curricula in twenty-three countries, Pergamon, Oxford.

Rossmiller, R.A. 1979, Resource utilization and productivity in IGE schools, Wisconsin University, Research and Development Center for Individualized Schooling. Abstract from ERIC database, item ED187714.

Saunders, P. 1991, 'The third edition of the test of understanding in college economics', Teaching College Economics, vol. 81, no. 2. pp. 32-37.

Saunders, P., G.L. Bach, J. D., Calderwood, W.L. Hansen, & Stein, H. 1984, A framework for teaching the basic concepts, 2nd edn, Joint Council on Economic Education, New York.

Schroeder, K. 1998, How girls know le$$, The Education Digest, vol. 63, no. 9. pp. 67-68 [online]. Available from ProQuest™ at URL: http://global.umi.com/pqdweb?TS=905734838&RQT=309&CC=1&Dtp=1&Did=000000029205862&Mtd=1& [Accessed 27 October 1998].

Sedaie, B. 1998, 'Economic literacy and the intention to attend college', Research in Higher Education, vol. 39, no. 3, pp. 337-364.

Sellin, N. 1990[1], PLSPATH Version 3.01, Program Manual. University of Hamburg, Hamburg, Germany.

Sellin, N. 1990[2], 'On aggregation bias' in The analysis of multivariate data in educational research: Studies of problems and their solutions, K.C Cheung, J.P. Keeves, N. Sellin & S.C. Tsoi, op. cit.

Shen, R. & Shen, T.Y. 1993, 'Economic thinking in China: Economic knowledge and attitudes of high school students', Journal of Economic Education, vol. 24, pp. 70-84.

Siegfried, J. J. & Meszaros, B.T. 1997, 'National voluntary content standards for pre-college economics education', AEA Papers and Proceedings, May, pp. 247-253.

Senior Secondary Assessment Board of South Australia, 1996 Economics Stage 1. Extended subject framework Business broad field of study, SSABSA, Adelaide.

Senior Secondary Assessment Board of South Australia, 1996 Economics Stage 2. Detailed syllabus statement. Business broad field of study, SSABSA, Adelaide.

Soper, J.C. & Walstad, W.B. 1987, Test of economic literacy. Examiner's manual, 2nd edn, Joint Council on Economic Education (now the National Council on Economic Education), New York.

Soper, J.C. 1978, The test of economic literacy. Forms A and B, Joint Council on Economic Education, New York.

Soper, J.C. 1979, The test of economic literacy: Discussion guide and rationale, Joint Council on Economic Education, New York.

Stock, P.A. & Rader, W.D. 1997, 'Level of economic understanding for senior high school students in Ohio', The Journal of Educational Research, vol. 91, no. 1, pp. 60-63.

Tasmanian Secondary Assessment Board 1998, 12 EC851/850C, 11/12 EC741/740 B, Economics, 11/12 EC903 A The Australian economy [online]. Available at URL: http://www.tassab.tased.edu.au/www/tassab.html.

TEU 1964, Test of economic understanding, Science Research Associates Inc., Chicago.

WA Economic syllabus - D304 syllabus

Walstad, W.B. & Becker, W.E. 1994, 'Achievement differences on multiple-choice and essay tests in economics. Research on economics education', American Economics Association Papers and Proceedings, vol. 84 no. 2, pp. 193-196.

Walstad, W.B. & Robson, D. 1997, 'Differential item functioning and male-female differences on multiple-choice tests in economics', Journal of Economic Education, Spring, pp. 155-171.

Walstad, W.B. & Watts, M. 1994, 'Economic education in secondary schools in the United States and other nations', International Journal of Social Education, vol. 8, no. 3, pp. 77-86.

Walstad, W.B. 1988, 'Economic literacy in the schools. The challenge of competition in a world economy', Speech delivered at the Press Colloqui on Economic Education at the American Economic Association, December. Vital Speeches of the Day, pp. 327-388.

Whitehead, D.J. & Halil, T. 1991, 'Economic literacy in the United Kingdom and the United States: A comparative study', Journal of Economic Education, Spring, pp. 101-110.

Wolf, R.M. 1997, 'Rating scales' in Educational research, methodology and measurement: An international handbook ed. J.P Keeves, Pergamon Press, Oxford, pp. 958-965.

Subject Index

Ingmar Wienen

Impact of Religion on Business Ethics in Europe and the Muslim World

Islamic versus Christian Tradition
2nd, revised edition

Frankfurt/M., Berlin, Bern, New York, Paris, Wien, 1999.
175 pp., num. fig., tab. and graf.
ISBN 3-631-34537-2 · pb. DM 65.–*
US-ISBN 0-8204-4314-X

This research project assesses the extent to which religion influences standards and behaviour in business, by comparing Islamic banking to co-operative banking as carried out by both Christians and Muslims. The study argues that Islamic banks are particular in the kind of products they offer, namely the *Islamic financial instruments*. On the other hand, it is the *organisation* which is key to co-operative banks. An empirical investigation of over 100 banks has revealed that *Islamic banks* are conventional banks with a product range modified according to Islamic religious law. *Co-operative banks* operate so as 'to help the poor', an objective in line with both Islamic and Christian ethics. The book demonstrates that Muslims and Christians can work together to foster development and to overcome poverty by referring to common ethical standards in business.

Contents: Problem definition and research objectives · State-of-the-art review: intercultural studies, studies on religions, studies on ethics and on business ethics · Theoretical study: "Europe" and the "Muslim World", rights and wrongs in Islam and Christianitiy, two ethical modes of operations · Plans, methods and means of research · Empirical study: Islamic banking in Europe, Islamic banking in the Muslim world, co-operative banking in Europe, co-operative banking in the Muslim world

Frankfurt/M · Berlin · Bern · New York · Paris · Wien
Distribution: Verlag Peter Lang AG
Jupiterstr. 15, CH-3000 Bern 15
Fax (004131) 9402131
*incl. value added tax
Prices are subject to change without notice.